Ed,

Here's to a
market cap! Enjoy...

Praise for *Talent Valuation*

"Tom draws on his unique background spanning senior roles in operations, finance, and human resources to deliver a thoughtful and comprehensive solution to talent valuation. It stands alone in this space, because he truly understands key value drivers."

—**Jack Stahl**, Corporate Board Member, Private Equity Advisor, and former CEO of Revlon and President of The Coca-Cola Company

"A captivating piece of work. Human resources is rapidly changing and becoming a much more data-intensive field. Tom McGuire's work infuses the study of HR with principles from finance and analytics. A compelling and important read for HR managers and general managers alike."

—**Mitchell Hoffman**, University of Toronto, Rotman School of Management

"Since the 1980s, whether in Finance, Marketing, or HR roles, Tom has always thought way beyond the curve—and delivered results. He collects and connects dots from all his experiences habitually. In this pioneering exposition on the value of talent, he connects them all."

—**Cynthia McCague**, Corporate Board Member and former SVP Human Resources at The Coca-Cola Company

"Linda has an uncanny way of drawing the line from concept to reality. She's smart and strategic and works hard to understand the challenges and goals of the business. This and her deep experience working with clients across industries makes her the ideal partner for Tom in helping link business value to talent."

—**Scott Katz**, Director-Talent Management, Turner Broadcasting

"This is unlike any other Human Resources book you have ever read! Tom and Linda deliver a scientific, yet practical, approach to understanding how to value your people and the intellectual capital they generate for the business. If you truly believe that people are your most important asset—this is a must-read."

—**Dave Sutton**, CEO, TopRight Partners and Coauthor, *Enterprise Marketing Management: The New Science of Marketing*

Talent Valuation

Accelerate Market Capitalization through Your Most Important Asset

Thomas McGuire
with Linda Brenner

Publisher: Paul Boger
Editor-in-Chief: Amy Neidlinger
Acquisitions Editor: Charlotte Maiorana
Operations Specialist: Jodi Kemper
Cover Designer: Alan Clements
Managing Editor: Kristy Hart
Project Editor: Elaine Wiley
Copy Editor: Chrissy White
Proofreader: Katie Matejka
Indexer: Lisa Stumpf
Compositor: Nonie Ratcliff
Manufacturing Buyer: Dan Uhrig

© 2015 by Thomas McGuire
Upper Saddle River, New Jersey 07458

For information about buying this title in bulk quantities, or for special sales opportunities (which may include electronic versions; custom cover designs; and content particular to your business, training goals, marketing focus, or branding interests), please contact our corporate sales department at corpsales@pearsoned.com or (800) 382-3419.

For government sales inquiries, please contact governmentsales@pearsoned.com.

For questions about sales outside the U.S., please contact international@pearsoned.com.

Company and product names mentioned herein are the trademarks or registered trademarks of their respective owners.

Printed in the United States of America

First Printing March 2015

ISBN-10: 0-13-400968-1
ISBN-13: 978-0-13-400968-1

Pearson Education LTD.
Pearson Education Australia PTY, Limited.
Pearson Education Singapore, Pte. Ltd.
Pearson Education Asia, Ltd.
Pearson Education Canada, Ltd.
Pearson Educación de Mexico, S.A. de C.V.
Pearson Education—Japan
Pearson Education Malaysia, Pte. Ltd.

Library of Congress Control Number: 2014959455

Contents

Acknowledgments

I want to thank my entire family, especially Chris, for once again allowing me to isolate myself more than usual during the last year. Special thanks also goes out to all of the mentors/leaders who gave me the opportunity to learn from so many experiences over the past 35-plus years: Rodolfo, Jeff, Ken, Jack, Charlie, Murray, Pat, Doug, Sergio, Cynthia, Vinita, Mike, Heinz, Ronald, Glen, Ted, David, Ceree, and no doubt others that I have unintentionally omitted.

—TM

About the Authors

Tom McGuire is unique in the talent management world as a person who has been both a Chief Financial Officer and a Global Talent Acquisition Director at well-known consumer product, NYSE companies.

Tom has 35 years of business experience following his first job out of college as a Peace Corps Volunteer in Central America. He began his business career as an external auditor in Columbus, Ohio, and after becoming a C.P.A. in 1982, left Coopers & Lybrand to join The Coca-Cola Company.

Tom spent his first years at Coke travelling around the world as an international auditor, followed by Corporate Finance roles supporting Latin America, Europe, and Africa. He assumed the Finance leadership role in the company's German Division in 1990 following the fall of the Berlin Wall. After playing a key role expanding Coke's business into the former East Germany, Tom returned to Atlanta in 1993 to work as part of the marketing management team reporting to the Chief Marketing Officer, Sergio Zyman. In addition to managing marketing financial plans, Tom was responsible for re-branding the World of Coca-Cola and Company Stores, building the WOCC Las Vegas and expanding the licensed merchandise business of the company. As a Vice-President in Coke's Marketing Division, Tom played a key role negotiating worldwide advertising agreements that led the way in establishing the industry trend towards fee-based compensation with agencies. From 1997 to 1999 Tom led the Global Talent Acquisition function at Coca-Cola, sourcing general management and marketing talent for worldwide operations and all talent for North America. In 1999 he moved into a role in Latin America, leading the development of a market-level strategy and integration plan for Peru following Coke's acquisition of Inca Cola.

In 2000 Tom joined Zyman Marketing Group in Atlanta, a developer of web-based marketing tools, as Chief Operating Officer. Following Zyman Marketing Group he formed a consulting venture, Human Capital Formation, LLC. In this business Tom provided consulting services that guided the redesign of the human resources functions and processes at clients including Children's Healthcare of Atlanta and Emory Healthcare.

In 2003, Tom joined Revlon, Inc., in New York City, serving as Revlon's Chief Financial Officer and then as President, Revlon International. During his tenure at Revlon, Tom led multiple debt and equity financing transactions totaling more than $2 billion, built the company's investor relations function, and implemented procedures to comply with Sarbanes-Oxley and other SEC mandated reporting requirements.

Tom rejoined the Coca-Cola Company in October 2007 as Group Director, Global Talent Acquisition, and focused on supporting the company's growth by developing and executing strategies to acquire top professional talent and independent contractors in the company's markets around the world. He built a globally based internal search firm at Coke and designed and implemented systematic measurement of talent quality for external hiring.

Tom retired from Coca-Cola and has worked with the Designs on Talent team since 2013. He also continues to own and operate Human Capital Formation, LLC.

He and his wife Chris have been married 33 years and have 3 children: Olivia, Sean, and Patrick. In his free time Tom enjoys road biking, playing guitar and other instruments, and writing and recording music.

tom@designsontalent.com

Linda Brenner started Designs on Talent (www.designsontalent. com) in 2004 with the vision of helping business leaders improve talent results. She then founded Skillsify, Inc. (www.skillsify.com) in 2011 as a way to scale and improve hiring and retention results through web-based, scalable, and measurable applications. The firms' clients include great brands such as Coca-Cola, IHG, Amazon, Expedia, The Home Depot, Chick-fil-A, L'Oreal, Microsoft and Turner Broadcasting.

Linda's innovative, results-oriented approach is coupled with a bias for action and a focus on measurable results. This same orientation is reflected throughout her team of talent acquisition, talent management, and finance experts.

Prior to founding Designs on Talent, Linda spent her professional career leading talent acquisition and talent management teams for Gap, Pepsi/Pizza Hut, and The Home Depot. Linda had a variety of roles at The Home Depot, including responsibility for company-wide OD initiatives such as succession planning, talent review, and 360° feedback. She then was tapped to lead the company's retail talent acquisition centralization effort. In addition to centralizing TA for the first time in the company's history, under Linda's leadership, The Home Depot also became the largest government contractor in the U.S. and forged first-of-their-kind partnerships with AARP, the Department of Defense, and the Department of Labor.

Prior to The Home Depot, Linda was with the Pizza Hut organization when it was still part of the Pepsi enterprise. There, she held a variety of roles, including HR generalist, national staffing manager, and the division's training and development group leader. At Gap, early in her career, she held operational roles in the Northeast division, including running the highest volume store there, until she moved to the company's San Francisco headquarters to lead a management development effort aimed at improving store performance.

Over the years, Linda has demonstrated a unique ability to break complex problems into manageable pieces and has led many teams to drive results in a timely, measurable, and results-oriented way. She works closely with business leaders and HR partners to create the business case, consensus, and tactical plan for change.

Linda holds a Master of Arts degree in Labor and Employment Relations and a Bachelor of Arts degree in Judaic Studies, both from University of Cincinnati. She and her family live in Atlanta.

linda@designsontalent.com

Chapter Summaries

Introduction

The Dow Jones Industrial Average has quadrupled over the last 20 years to an underlying market capitalization exceeding $4.6 trillion.[1] More than eighty percent of the change in market capitalization, excluding oil reserves, is accounted for by an increase of nearly $2.7 trillion in intellectual capital value.[2] There is only one source of intellectual capital—and that's talent.

Chapter 1: Important vs. Critical Talent: What if the Beatles Had Been a Company?

All people in an organization are important, but some drive significant business value, and for these the human capital strategy and investment must vary. This chapter gives background to the model we use to determine critical roles and introduces the Beatles as an example for differentiating critical from simply important talent.

Chapter 2: Is Your Most Important Asset Really an Asset?

HR speak is often riddled with slogans—and "people are our most important asset" is one that has been adopted by business leaders everywhere. But is it true that people are *literally* your most important asset? Accounting guidance and commentary from *competent authority* is reviewed to present some surprising conclusions.

Chapter 3: Valuing and Evaluating Companies and Their Intellectual Capital

Our proprietary method for calculating the value of intellectual capital for public companies is a novel—and meaningful—way to evaluate companies. Using information available to the public (such as financial reports required by the SEC), trends among industries and results between companies within industries are compared in order to understand the dynamics of intellectual capital. Examples of recording intellectual capital in the event of acquisition are highlighted here. Technical issues in working with this information are discussed for those who want to dive in deeper. The reader learns that intellectual capital can exceed 90% of the market value for companies in certain industries and that human capital is the unique source of that value.

Chapter 4: Understanding Active and Inert Components of Intellectual Capital

This chapter delves into the dynamic of creating, sustaining, and growing intellectual capital. With the exception of human capital, all intellectual capital is in fact inert and cannot sustain itself, grow, or evolve. Inert intellectual capital: A brand, patent, or proprietary process or technology accumulates over time and depends solely on the output of the "active" component of intellectual capital—human capital. The creation of intellectual capital and its actual components is illustrated for multiple companies in this section.

Chapter 5: Identifying Critical Roles Through Work Processes

Once the intellectual capital of an entity is understood, action must be taken to create, sustain, and grow it. This action begins with pinpointing the roles that are critical and must therefore command the focus of talent strategy. Here the reader identifies and prioritizes *structural* human capital needs by analyzing critical success factors and the work processes that achieve them. Examples of intellectual capital and what is considered critical to producing it are drawn from investor presentations and other data from a number of Fortune 500 companies. These examples serve to illustrate the starting point for prioritizing human capital.

Chapter 6: The New Talent Strategy Game Plan

Human capital strategy is ultimately driven by understanding critical needs and the availability of talent to satisfy them. Depending on the facts and circumstances for any given situation, choosing between building talent internally, hiring from the outside, or borrowing talent on a contingent basis is a critical consideration. While the "build versus buy" framework is a more common one, contingent (temporary/contract) talent at the professional level will play a more important part of the human capital mix in the future. Because many of the characteristics of using contingent talent are similar to when a company uses debt rather than equity to finance a given transaction, debt versus equity is used as an analogy for the reader to apply when considering the pluses and minuses of this talent alternative.

Chapter 7: The Only Metric that Matters

If a smaller group of value-producing roles drives most of the market value by creating, sustaining and growing intellectual capital, how can the success of talent strategies and investments targeting this group be measured? What are the metrics that have the greatest impact on the outcome of business investments and accumulated value? Can something as abstract as the quality of talent even be measured? How important is talent quality to value creation? What drivers affect the talent quality of hiring and retention efforts? In a world of intellectual capital value, a discussion and conclusion about talent quality is imperative, as is a path to metrics that organizations can start using today.

Chapter 8: Attracting and Retaining the Human Capitalist Investor

Human capital is different from labor; your top talent should be thought of in the same way as investors you woo to buy your company's stock. Their interests are similar. But the "personnel" department of old still exists in many organizations and is ill equipped to deal with this new breed of *human capitalist investor*. Taking a page from Investor Relations, a model already exists that can be applied and reinvented in the Human Resources functions of innovative organizations reliant on intellectual capital.

Chapter 9: Looking Back and Looking Forward

Market value creation has almost entirely changed across industries in the past 35 years without a corresponding change in understanding the resources that create value. The opportunity exists to gain meaningful competitive advantage in this environment, and the value in doing so is difficult to overstate. The financial profession has proposed research to address disclosure of intangible assets that do not appear on financial statements and the underlying human capital that produce them. When will companies be required to disclose and what should they do in the meantime?

Chapter 10: Who Is Responsible? What Is the Purpose of HR?

Many entrepreneurs and start-up CEOs have a visceral reaction to the notion of hiring a "Human Resources" team. They equate such employees with an onslaught of bureaucracy and adminstrivia. But at what point in an emerging organization's growth cycle should a *human capital* team be assembled? What is the greatest value that can be generated through people? Is the Human Resources function, as it exists, capable of leading the change? The development—and evolution—of a measurable talent strategy that supports the business plan for growth is the ultimate (and arguably singular) purpose of a new breed of human capital professionals.

Endnotes

1. Dow Jones Industrial Average Fact Sheet, as of July 31, 2014.

2. The dollar increase of $2.7 trillion is shown net of increase in the value of energy companies in the DJIA. Reserves of energy companies are the other significant asset that is not recorded at market value on the books of the owners due to accounting regulations. This net number represents the estimated change in intellectual capital value.

Foreword

Business books about managing human capital are not new. Writing about how to manage, inspire, and engage employees is as old as industry. But the subject of those books is typically focused on HR functional practices or individual management methods. In such contexts, much has been written about the struggle to fund costly HR programs—as well as positing that investing in people is critical, yet being unable to prove its value.

This book is unlike one you've ever read about human capital management.

The fact is, during the lifetime of the average senior executive today, the world's developed economies have shifted from being primarily industrial to primarily knowledge-driven. In the industrial work of making and moving things, workers served machines. In today's knowledge and service work however, machines serve workers. Knowledge workers (rather than capital assets) are the means of production in a knowledge economy, which is what we now have.

On this basis, it seems entirely reasonable that businesses wonder what the valuation and return on investment are for their means of production. But because of the speed with which these changes have occurred, paradigms and behaviors of organizations have not shifted sufficiently to recognize and deal with new facts regarding people. Measurement systems that will support this new reality have not been discovered yet. That's not surprising. Employees outwardly appear pretty much the same regardless of whether they serve or are served by machines. As human beings, they have many of the same needs in a business environment as they did before. But what is needed to manage the human aspect of a business to create sustainable economic value has certainly changed.

Human Resources professionals are impacted more than most by the shift to a knowledge economy. Although there are still remnants out there, the function has finally fled its former designation as the "Personnel Department," but is presently wavering on a new name. After evolving to Human Resources and then having second thoughts, many organizations are trying out "People Function" led by a "Chief People Officer" and staffed with a team of "Human Resource Business Partners." Simply changing titles is arguably ineffective, but the trend is revealing in terms of how organizations are grappling to understand new management requirements.

The fact is, the economic relevance of people has changed and become more complex. In the last 35 years, the knowledge worker came into existence while labor roles were significantly reduced. At the same time, the role of service worker—somewhere in between knowledge worker and laborer—emerged to provide key support in roles ranging from customer service to installation and other assistance of all kinds, typically leveraging technology.

During this same time period, HR has adapted organizationally, but in essence its orientation to how people create market value remains deficient. HR teams have changed their titles, role definitions, and organizational structure to Shared Services, Centers of Excellence, and HR Business Partners, but the work that gets done (while streamlined) hasn't fundamentally changed. As often as not, adapting organizationally has been a cost cutting exercise—in the face of increasing stakes for human capital. Companies struggle to define success measures for HR, so the function remains untethered to business outcomes.

Yet the reason for being in business has not changed. Creating value for shareholders remains the reason for organizing as a for-profit business. What has changed is how that value is created.

How value is created in a knowledge economy and the implications of this on managing talent is the focus of this book. The product of knowledge workers is intellectual capital. Knowledge workers own "human capital," which are the skills and qualifications that enable productivity above and beyond that of unskilled labor. Unlike physical capital, human capital cannot be bought; it is owned by the knowledge worker. In this respect, the knowledge worker is more an investor (you'll soon see) than an employee.

One reality of a company powered by human capital is that certain roles and functions are more critical to business outcomes than others. The types of roles and functions that are most critical tend to vary by industry, as the intellectual capital they produce is largely industry-specific. This is one of the many unrecognized and misunderstood challenges that face HR functions across the board: reconciling the idea that everyone is important but some talent is more critical than others. This notion seems contrary to the HR ethos when discussed. Nevertheless, connecting the dots between intellectual capital and talent bears this fact out. As such, investing disproportionately in the most critical talent will optimize business success.

Another reality of a company powered by human capital is that quality is the talent measurement that matters most. The productivity of a "star" performer is exponentially higher than the productivity of an "average" one. The value of human capital increases as more "star" performers are hired and retained and, in turn, they produce more intellectual capital for the company. Therefore, talent quality must be measured and managed, especially for critical roles.

Against that backdrop of change, it's not surprising that the workforce itself has evolved significantly. With intellectual capital emerging as the value driver, but with constant economic pressure on businesses to become more efficient, the churn of reorganization and downsizing seems endless. Indeed, employment is less "permanent" than it was in the past, and the workforce has begun to adapt to that reality. Although people have generally accepted the fact that they will have multiple employers during their working lives, many of them have opted to cut ties with "permanent" employment entirely. The contingent workforce, those who contract work on a shorter-term basis, has grown by leaps and bounds. Arguably fueled to some extent by those who were initial victims of downsizing, the voluntary segment of this workforce has taken root and is quickly growing.

This new segmentation of the workforce provides businesses with both challenges and opportunities. The growing voluntary segment of contingent talent is often highly skilled and in demand. Businesses must determine the best approach to strategically fit this talent into its workforce plan. After all, ignoring this challenge—or continuing to "outsource" this responsibility to the Purchasing Department—is to ignore a highly competent and critical source of talent. Becoming proficient at integrating contingent talent provides businesses with additional flexibility in their human capital structure, an attribute that will continue to be important in the foreseeable future.

It is not surprising that talent, particularly those most in demand, see themselves for what they are: the new capital...the means of production...as investors rather than employees. "Human capitalist investors" bring capital to the business, and they have different ways of thinking about the expected returns than the laborers of days gone by.

The magnitude of this socio-economic change is so sweeping and fundamental to value creation that it requires the attention and stewardship of all leaders; it cannot be delegated to a single function. Although there is important work for the Human Resources function to do and a critical place to which the function must evolve, business leadership teams must usher the way forward. At the same time, they must recognize that they've entered uncharted territory. The systems and roles that enable efficient and effective human capital deployment don't exist yet, but we predict they soon will. This book is intended to stoke imaginations as to what the future of human capital management might give rise to. What are the limits to accelerating market capitalization through our most valuable asset?

—Linda Brenner

Introduction

Market cap growth in the twenty-first century has evolved and become a function of human capital productivity. As recently as 1980, the difference between book value and market value for the average U.S. corporation was not significant. However, by the year 2000, the average company's market value exceeded book value by about 75%.[1] This excess value that the market placed on the average company's share price was for the most part attributable to the value of intangible assets, specifically intellectual capital in the form of brands, trademarks, patents, and other proprietary inventions and commercial secrets. In fact, a quadrupling of the Dow Jones Industrial Average over the last 20 years to a market capitalization of $4.6 trillion is a testimony to the "age of the knowledge worker." More than 80% of the increased value of the Dow over that time period, excluding oil reserves, is accounted for by an increase in intellectual capital value amounting to $2.7 trillion.[2]

Tangible asset intensive businesses such as Bethlehem Steel have given way to intangible asset giants like Microsoft, represented in the DJIA. General Motors and Goodyear have been overshadowed in favor of the likes of Pfizer and Visa. The percentage of value represented by intellectual capital climbs as knowledge workers produce intangible assets, which in turn accelerate cash flow.

All successful consumer products, pharmaceutical, and technology companies have followed this trend and have value that is vastly larger than reported net assets, reflecting the size of their unrecorded intellectual capital (for example, the brand values of Apple and

Coca-Cola) and the productivity of their knowledge workers. As an example, at a mid-sized consumer products company I worked for, we borrowed many millions of dollars during my tenure, collateralized purely by valuable intangible assets that were owned but not recorded on the books. On a smaller scale, the venture capitalist who funded a startup I was part of secured their entire investment with a $10 million life insurance policy on the namesake founder! Large or small, the value of modern entities hinges on the intellectual capital they own and the people that produce it.

Is the market simply over-valuing intangible assets today, or has it perhaps under-valued them historically? Do certain businesses literally own something of value that they did not own in the past? If so, how was it acquired? Is this real or just a bubble waiting to burst?

Let's take a few steps back. In 1960, a mid-level executive (say, age 40) would have entered the business world in the early 1940s. By 1980, a mid-level executive would have entered the business world in the early 1960s. By 2000, of course, a mid-level executive would have entered the business world in the early 1980s. College graduates in the U.S. population in 1940, 1960, and 1980 totaled approximately 6, 13, and 55 million people, respectively—almost a ten-fold increase over that period of time. The growth rate for male college grads in each of those years shows even sharper relative increases than for the general population (the workforce was less diverse than today). This steep curve in higher education provided the source for enterprise value above and beyond that produced by manual labor to industries in the U.S. and around the world. This intellectual value, deconstructed, takes the form of patents, trademarks, brands, proprietary processes (managerial and industrial), and proprietary technologies. Let's put it this way: With the unprecedented breakthrough levels of participation in higher education (and the investment to accomplish this), the results were certainly going to be dramatically valuable—and those results are the knowledge worker and human capital.

The market today is not simply over-valuing companies. Valuation boils down to projecting a company's ability to produce future cash flow. The majority of capital deployed to produce cash flow in many of today's most highly valued enterprises is intellectual capital. Although investors recognize this intellectual capital in the price they pay for shares, its value does not currently appear in financial statements and reports.

Although the focus of this book is on how to form and accumulate human capital (the sole source of all intellectual capital), it will also predict the future of and make the case for providing investors with sufficient information regarding a company's ability to do so. The need to understand and manage human capital, and thereby grow intellectual capital, is not optional—it is essential. It will happen efficiently or inefficiently, and it will certainly define competitive advantage; there will be winners and losers.

One of the key takeaways from this book is that talent and value creation in today's world are virtually synonymous. The challenge is how to methodically, rather than haphazardly, understand and manage this direct relationship between talent and value creation for the benefit of shareholders.

This challenge is addressed using examples of value created in a variety of industries. How it is created and what the implications are from a talent strategy perspective are explained. Prioritization techniques are applied to highlight which roles are critical versus simply important, or even unnecessary. Many companies state they want top quality talent in all roles. This is understandable; if a position is worth having in an organization, it is certainly worth filling with a quality resource. However, in a world of limited resources, decisions must be made regarding where and how to invest. What is imperative about creating value is that talent in critical roles be thought of differently.

By the time a critical need exists, it is often too late to optimize the outcome unless there is a pipeline of talent ready. Once the need exists, compromises must be made, and compromise destroys value (particularly related to quality). Ensuring that talent is immediately available for every role in an organization is impractical, expensive, and unnecessary. However, I want to guide readers to understand that, regardless of cost, being able to identify those "no compromise" roles and to make the necessary talent investments is inexpensive relative to the value gained.

For example, it's good to have quality talent in the role of Accounts Receivable Director (after all, you haven't completed the sale until you have the cash!), but it is probably not essential to have a ready pipeline of internal and external candidates to fill the Accounts Receivable Director role in the future. Although the role is important, it is largely administrative in nature, and talent can be quickly sourced when needed. On the other hand, if you are a pharmaceutical company, you are most likely dependent on top-notch research talent for a sizeable chunk of your present and future market value, and the cost of building and maintaining a pipeline for such critical roles may be the best money you ever spend.

Talent in these critical roles is certainly part of a company's capital—its human capital. Today's business opportunities require investing both financial and human capital to bear fruit. For that reason similar management routines and infrastructure are needed for both types of capital. Characteristics that human capital and financial capital have in common and how those similarities can lead to practices that improve human capital management are discussed later in this book.

The impact of talent on value creation is an economic fact for all enterprises. Years before the enormous effect of human capital began showing up in market capitalization, the case was plainly stated by Economics Nobel Laureate Milton Friedman: "The return on human capital is superior to that on financial capital."[3] Suffice it to say that companies require both kinds of capital in today's knowledge driven world to be successful—financial capital to place the bet, and human capital to win it.

The economics are clear, but current accounting rules fall short in not allowing internally developed intellectual capital to be recorded on the books. This accounting shortfall contributes materially to an information gap for companies and investors alike and has a negative impact on the chain of metrics driving sustainable value creation. There are signs that the accounting limitations will eventually be solved, but this will take years and is dependent on the agendas set by regulatory authorities and the accounting profession. Although the Financial Accounting Standards Board (FASB) had circulated a project proposal to establish standards for disclosing intangible assets not recognized in financial statements, other priorities took precedent, and it is unclear when this issue will ultimately begin to be addressed.

Notwithstanding the uncertain timeframe for mandated disclosure requirements and despite the significance of the value, most companies have substantial internal limitations to refining their management of intangible asset creation. Although the role of people in the value equation has clearly changed from "enabling" to being the "means of production," internal ability to deal with the scale of this change is woefully inadequate. Human capital is still more a buzzword than it is an asset managed with the diligence and deference accorded to tangible capital investment in a past era.

Finance has historically been the lynchpin in connecting the means of production with economic decision-making and consequences. As a soulmate of manufacturing operations, an entire financial practice grew up with Cost Accounting nearly becoming a separate profession. As of now, the relationship between Finance and HR does not reflect the new reality. The relationship is mostly an administrative one. Although I feel it is safe to predict that a similar role for Finance exists with respect to human capital as has existed with manufacturing capital, it is unclear how this role will evolve. Guidance related to fostering this relationship is provided in the final chapter.

Culturally, HR departments are not well prepared to tackle the issue of critical versus noncritical roles wherein certain talent is simply a higher priority than others. Because resources will always be limited, resolving this quandary is essential. Either limited resources are spread evenly across the organization or spending is tilted toward the highest value roles (in this context, spending includes everything from the cost of a recruiter to the merit increase pool). The challenge is how to create an environment where all people feel equally important as individuals and team members, yet recognize that specific roles have differing criticality and value depending on the company's products and industry. Easier said than done, but I'll attempt to bring this issue a bit more down to earth in the first chapter.

Endnotes

1. Giniat and Libert. *Value Rx: How to Make the Most of Your Organization's Assets and Relationships.* HarperBusiness, 2001.

2. The dollar increase of $2.7 trillion is shown net of increase in the value of energy companies in the DJIA. Reserves of energy companies are the other significant asset that is not recorded at market value on the books of the owners due to accounting regulations. This net number represents the estimated value of change in intellectual capital value.

3. *Free to Choose*, Milton & Rose Friedman, Harcourt Brace Jovanovich, 1980.

1

Important vs. Critical Talent: What if the Beatles Had Been a Company?

- *Connecting goals, critical success factors, and results*
- *Jobs that are important but not critical*
- *Allocating limited resources in a high impact way*

I have to begin with a short story, before getting to the Beatles, about the evolution of a mindset: my mindset on talent. It's a story about Coca-Cola and Germany during the fall of the Berlin Wall and a mid-career CPA from Ohio. The experience I had in Germany with Coke, before ever having been in an HR role, set in motion a series of experiences that led me to an entirely new perspective about the value of talent to organizations operating in our modern economy.

Leading the Finance organization in 1993 at Coca-Cola's German Division, one of the company's largest businesses outside the U.S., I was tapped to pilot a new enterprise business model that was being tested in a few locations around the world. The intent of the enterprise model was to bring focus to the factors most critical to achieving the company's stated goals and to document in detail how the work required by each of those critical factors was performed. By understanding these elements, we could make better decisions to evolve structure, close gaps, streamline work, and invest in the organization and information systems.

I had just spent nearly three years as part of the management team that rapidly invested half a billion dollars in the former East Germany, and we had captured a clear lead in the non-alcoholic beverage market. We were successful in part because of the infrastructure we already had on the ground in West Germany. Our scale and resources in the West were a clear advantage, as were our relationships with key customers who also wanted to develop the East, and our production capabilities, particularly in one-way packages.

On the other hand, our organization was rigid. For example, the people on my finance team had been in the same roles for an average of 19 years. They were very, very good at what they did, but not so good at what they didn't do. We had unlimited opportunity in the East, but our organization's flexibility was limited. Our German organization needed a way to evolve but was culturally change-adverse. For these reasons, we were an ideal choice to pilot a model that facilitated structural change and did so by involving people and connecting to business outcomes.

A key aspect of the model required us to rank critical success factors according to their importance to achieving business goals. Critical success factors (CSFs), defined as those things that must be done well in order for the business to succeed, generally ran along organization lines (for example, the marketing organization). Sometimes however, multiple functions in the organization might contribute to achieving a particular CSF, depending on the work required. It was a humbling, yet revealing, experience to discover that financial management ended up near the bottom of the ranking among 16 CSFs in terms of importance to achieving our company goals. Of course all CSFs are "critical," but some are just more critical and value adding than others. Enhancing the Coke trademark, to no one's surprise, outranked financial management as a factor critical to success.

At that time, I had been a member of Coke's Finance team for 11 years and found this conclusion disconcerting and almost embarrassing. However, the analysis made it crystal clear that this was indeed the case. It followed that although everyone in the organization was important (myself included, I hoped), certain people were in roles that, by design, contributed significantly more value than others as defined by their relative impact on achieving the company's goals. The more value-adding roles of course were concentrated in those parts of the organization that drove the highest-ranking critical success factors.

The outcome of this experience was the objective, even inarguable, conclusion that some roles are more valuable to the business than others. But that is a difficult position for many to adopt. Even my reaction to learning how low Finance ranked—one of near-embarrassment—indicates how deeply-seated our idea of equality and fairness is to the culture of work.

Which brings us to the Beatles.

In search of a way to remove the sociological barriers to thinking about talent and equality, the Fab Four popped into my mind as a way to objectively achieve that end. The rock-and-roll band that changed the world of music forever in just eight years and sold more than 600 million records certainly did not do all of that work alone. There were managers, producers, recording engineers, and even the guitar tuners.

Imagine how many times guitars needed to be tuned over the course of hundreds of live concerts. There is no doubt that the role of guitar tuner was essential to the band's sound and brand. In fact, the tuner may have technically been a better guitar player than any one of the Beatles themselves. But they weren't a Beatle. John, Paul, George and Ringo were. And although it is a very important job and not an easy one to do, there are probably tens of thousands of people in the world that would have been qualified to professionally tune a guitar. And certainly, the band greatly appreciated and valued their skill and service. But for the Beatles as a business, critical success factors centered on performing, song writing, music distribution, and public relations.

Certainly, the fellows who so expertly tuned the guitars would not have kept their jobs for long if they hadn't fit in well with the rest of the Beatles' crew, didn't get the job done expertly and on time, and couldn't be relied on to help make the whole venture work. I assume they got paid at least as well as others who did similar work; in fact, it is likely they worked, as needed, for multiple client bands. I guess you could say the same for all the individuals who packed and moved and unpacked the Beatles equipment as well. They all were important in the same way I was important as a Finance leader at Coke.

I definitely felt important as a newly minted CPA when I first joined Coca-Cola in 1982. It was a dream company for me; plenty of things to be proud of and everyone always seemed to enjoy hearing about "how Coca-Cola was doing." What a great company to be associated with! But realistically, what I did was important although not really unique in any particular way. I wasn't tasked with inventing a lot of intellectual capital or things investors would ultimately pay a lot of money for. My role was important, but a whole lot of people could probably have done my job. The fact remains, if someone else had done my job and performed either 25% better or 25% worse than me over all those years, the impact on the price of the stock would have been negligible in either case.

That is not to say that my job was not important, that it did not have to be done well, that I was overpaid, or that performing 25% better than average wasn't a good idea. But I trusted—even took for granted—that others in the organization would ensure Coca-Cola's relevance to consumers, that we would continue to innovate (Diet Coke, Fruitopia, Power-aide, Simply Juices, and Coke Zero were all introduced during my tenure) and that we would outpace our competitors. I had no doubt that McDonald's would continue to serve only Coca-Cola products and remain our largest single customer in the world.

All of this was worth its weight in gold to me at cocktail parties and weekend neighborhood barbecues. If the people behind all of those efforts couldn't sustain and grow the business, it could severely damage my valuable social currency. On a subtler note, I hadn't believed that my comrades in the Finance organization, despite their best efforts, could have had the same impact on the value of stock in my IRA and, eventually, my stock options as those creating the magic with brands and consumers. Supporting their work from a financial standpoint was well worth it to me.

Still, in spite of all I experienced and the objective analysis I eventually led in Germany, I can understand how difficult it is for business leaders, particularly Human Resource professionals, to think about some roles (and the people in them) as being more valuable than others. So rather than over-investing in the acquisition and retention of these key skills, organizations typically opt to spread limited resources equally across the organization. Examples abound:

- One HR Business Partner per function or per "x" number of employees
- One approach to recruiting across disparate disciplines
- One set of salary ranges by job level across varied functions
- Every employee participating in the same type of onboarding, training, and performance management efforts

Linda: So in your analogy, would it really matter to the Beatles if the guitar tuner quit? Or if they didn't have one?

Tom: They do need a tuner, which is why the role exists. You want the guitar tuner to stay if he's doing a good job; you need one, and there is value to continuity. But if he leaves, he can be replaced with relative ease. It would be inconvenient but would not impact the value of the "Beatles." Having said that, guitar manufacturers now sell self-tuning guitars. The guitars use built-in technology to automatically tune themselves more accurately and faster than a human being can. Clearly, there are parallels between self-tuning guitars and work automation in other industries that affect non-critical roles or ones which don't rely on human ingenuity. I would expect more of these examples in the future as robotics perform more and more tasks that do not require complex thinking, creativity, innovation, and other highly valued work. Bottom line, if the guitar tuner quit, it might be an inconvenience to the band, but it wouldn't be as devastating to the Beatles as if Paul quit.

Linda: I get it—but it still sounds callous. How do you expect the guitar tuner to be motivated and retained, knowing that he doesn't matter as much as the band members?

Tom: I, for one, would give my eyeteeth to be the Beatles' guitar tuner. Imagine being associated in such a way with a band like the Beatles! But putting the band's popularity aside, as long as he is paid fairly relative to other guitar tuners and recognized appropriately for his contributions, he would most likely stay and do his job well. There is a lot of psychic income available being part of a successful organization regardless of what role you play. On the tangible side of things, there is increased economic security as well.

But more importantly, I believe that employees actually understand their roles in the organization and how their positions are valued with respect to others. It could be perceived as disingenuous when messaging in a company indicates that all roles and people in them are equally valued. In reality, pay, benefits, and perks (if nothing else) tell a far different story about who is critically valuable to the business plan. Honesty and transparency about the business model is a better communication choice.

Last, if I were truly dissatisfied with my supporting role in the organization, I might take the leap and start up my own agency contracting out guitar tuners or giving music lessons or going head to head with Guitar Center. That is where I flip from being a supporting player to being a critical one.

A dramatic cultural change must take place for businesses to strategically connect investment in people with value creation.

All people are equally as important as individuals, but some are more critical to the business by virtue of the roles they play now and will play in the future. Given the importance of human capital to the valuation of businesses, the people strategy has to be focused on these roles to drive the most value.

Think about it: If the Beatles had been a typical company, everyone associated with the band (the roadies, producers, marketers, and the musicians themselves) would have received the same general approach to compensation, training, performance reviews, and so on. George and Ringo would have received engagement surveys, and their opinions about how well things were going would have carried the same weight as the guitar tuners'. And if Paul had quit, they might have just posted the job in the same way they might have advertised for a stage hand. With an equal approach to everyone and everything, the entire company would never have survived the Rolling Stones.

Back in Germany in 1993, we set out to understand how our most important goals were achieved by connecting critical success factors to the organization and, ultimately, to specific roles. The logic of this model stuck with me, and I had the opportunity years later to begin connecting the dots between financial value and talent decisions in a bigger and more measurable way when leading Global Talent Acquisition at Coke.

Linda: You talk a lot about "critical success factors"—can you explain how a company would determine what those are?

Tom: Critical success factors (CSF) are the things that must be done well in order to achieve goals. The CSF approach could be used generically. For example, profit and a measure of volume are common goals in any business, and you could determine CSFs relative to those goals.

In this book we focus the CSF construct on the creation of intellectual capital because it drives the market capitalization of most companies. There are several steps to this process:

1. Identifying the specific intellectual capital (IC) that is most important to creating value within a company.

2. Linking critical success factors to the specific intellectual capital being examined (we've highlighted CSFs for various companies throughout this book as examples)

3. Rating and ranking the contribution of each CSF to the specific IC. This is crucial because the top few will tend to disproportionately drive actual success or failure. These, then, are the CSFs that ultimately require the most robust and measurable talent plans.

Linda: I think many leaders might believe they could get to this same place without all the analysis. True?

Tom: In a lot of businesses, especially smaller and less complex ones, leaders might get 80% of this right simply through rigorous, guided discussion. However, systematically analyzing IC goals and ranking CSFs will uncover insights that may otherwise be missed. In some cases, a small margin of error could have significant impact on downstream decision-making and results. In larger and more complex businesses, the intuitive approach would yield even more dubious outcomes. A disciplined approach to the CSF construct will yield the most accurate talent decisions and, ultimately, business results.

2

Is Your Most Important Asset Really an Asset?

- *Defining "asset"*
- *Intellectual capital: The product of knowledge workers*
- *The Intellectual Capital Index (ICI) explained*

Are people in your organization really an asset or is that just a trendy slogan? If it feels like an asset it must be one, right? Perhaps. Historically, it was popular, especially in HR circles, to protest against thinking about people as merely assets. Articles teaming with pleas such as "...remember, your employees are someone's mother, father, or child," abounded, warning against a philosophy of ownership or even slavery of some sort. However, most HR professionals have now come to appreciate at least talking about people as "assets," although doing so conceptually, since people certainly cannot be owned. Is it a fair analogy? As we all know, accountants define what is or is not an "asset," and in fact, they do sometimes record assets that are not owned.

From an accounting standpoint, an asset is an economic resource that can be owned *or controlled* to produce value that can ultimately be converted into cash. So in some cases, simply controlling a resource permits, and indeed requires, recording it as an asset.

For example, a piece of equipment that is not owned, but only leased from its owner, must be recorded as an asset by the lessee if the lease agreement extends to 75% or more of the equipment's estimated useful life.[1] The lessee has both significant control over its productive deployment and an obligation for the economic cost.

Of course, no one would want to argue that a person is or should be, in effect, owned by their employer. However, there is a clear connection between the investment in knowledge workers and the lion's share of an entity's market value (see Chapters 3, 4, and 5). In addition, there is the exponential upside of retaining and safeguarding critical talent over a substantial number of years, which certainly encourages the thinking of people as bona fide assets. Last, it would be reasonable for a company to argue that it has significant control over the productive deployment of its human capital and a corresponding obligation to pay for its economic cost.

Whether or not we ever actually record human capital as an asset on a company's books, analysis indicates that investors already recognize and pay for human capital and other intellectual capital of a company when one compares market values to book values. *Consequently, over the last several decades the relevance of financial statements to understanding an entity's actual worth has greatly diminished.*

Linda: If investors already recognize it, then why don't companies have to report on the value of "intangible assets" driven by human capital?

Tom: First of all, in my opinion the quality of financial reporting has significantly increased over the last 20 years; just take a look at a company's Annual Report on Form 10-K from 1993 and compare it to a 2013 version. The disclosures are much more robust. Having said that, there is a long way to go before financial reporting alone provides a basis for making sound investment decisions (see our discussion of recent financial reporting developments in Chapter 9, "Looking Back and Looking Forward"). The mentality of the two main organizations that influence this area, the Financial Accounting Standards Board (FASB) and the U.S. Securities and Exchange Commission (SEC), is focused first and foremost on disclosing risk and protecting investors from the downside.

That mission leads to conservative accounting requirements complemented by a constant push to disclose risks that are not apparent in the accounting numbers. Conservative accounting requires an arms length transaction to evidence the value of assets. This does not accommodate intangible assets grown organically within a company—it does, however, support the recording of intangible assets (such as brands) if they are purchased from a seller. You could argue conservative accounting errs in the direction of understating assets and overstating liabilities in an effort to "protect" investors.

Paradoxically, the push to disclose risk is where we begin to see more information regarding the value of unrecorded intangible assets and human capital. It is in the early stages, but I believe this trend will continue and such information will become more useful to investors over time. Commentaries about intellectual property, R&D, and human capital are more and more often included among the "description of business," "discussion of risks," and "management discussion and analysis" sections of a company's 10-K. It is not standard, however, and largely free form, but the comments provide a glimpse of this trend nonetheless.

The SEC puts particular disclosure pressure on companies in the life science industries (biotechnology, pharmaceutical, etc.) since R&D expenditure and the potential value of patents are often the most significant considerations from an investor stand-point. Not surprisingly, as you will see in the next chapter, these companies are valued almost entirely on their intellectual capital.

The valuation of intangible assets, and by extension human capital, is rooted in expected future cash flow. Conservative accounting frowns on forward-looking statements, and future financial projections are largely taboo in financial reporting. This barrier discourages extensive discussion of these assets by public companies, which puts investors at a disadvantage, forcing them to research and estimate the impact on their own.

This fact is not lost on either the accounting profession or securities regulators. Former SEC chief, Steven Wallman, captured the following thoughts for an AICPA (American Institute of Certified Public Accountants) audience in a 1996 presentation:

> ...traditional financial statements are now significantly less reflective of the assets that create wealth than in times past. Intangible assets such as brand names, intellectual capital, patents, copyrights, human resources, etc., are generating an increasing amount of our overall wealth...With certain limited exceptions, such as the purchase of a brand name, these "soft" assets are not recognized in the financial statements. The primary obstacles relate to valuation difficulties, the inherent uncertainty of any value ultimately determined, and the resulting potential for fraud. As a result of these concerns, we attribute no value in financial reports to something as obviously significant as Disney's Mickey Mouse. This cannot be the correct result for the long-term utility of financial reporting.[2]

Well, who could argue with that? Mickey Mouse, Coke Zero, Tide, and Viagra certainly have great value even though it's not reflected on their companies' financial statements. Yet every time a share of their stock is traded, investors are paying for these and other intangible assets. Human capital, the contribution of knowledge workers in an organization, is an integral part of those intangible assets—in fact, the only active part, as you learn more about in Chapter 4, "Understanding Active and Inert Components of Intellectual Capital."

How can we get an *objective* view of what Steven Wallman was talking about with respect to assets that are not reflected on the traditional financial statements? These are the assets that people create, accumulate, and sustain utilizing their knowledge, experience, and skills...as well as the people themselves. This asset class can be defined as *intellectual capital* (IC).

Linda: What is the difference between intellectual capital and intangible assets?

Tom: Intellectual capital is a subset of intangible assets. Some notable intangible assets are not intellectual capital. For example, certain rights granted with respect to property, such as mineral exploration rights or right-of-way rights, are intangible assets but not intellectual capital. For the most part, however, the majority of intangible assets, both those on the books due to acquisition and those not on the books, are indeed intellectual capital.

Having become fascinated with the idea of IC as a percentage of overall enterprise value, what it means, and how it has changed over the years, I set out to find a way to isolate and analyze this value using public company information. I now believe this will be an increasingly important way for investors, candidates, business leaders, and others to evaluate businesses.

Here's how intellectual capital was isolated:

As a first step, the value of unrecorded intangible assets was determined by calculating the difference between a debt-free market value (enterprise value) and a debt-free shareholder's equity (book value) of the selected company. Market value for a public company is a calculation of shares issued and outstanding times the market price per share. Net debt is added to that number and to shareholder's equity from the 10-K to calculate what is referred to as *enterprise value* and *book value*.

The difference between enterprise value and book value is typically the value of unrecorded intangible assets in the form of intellectual capital (with some exceptions to this rule such as oil reserves of energy companies, discussed later in the book). These are the assets that are not deemed measurable or certain enough by accounting standards to be included on the books of the company. Yet for investors, they are a solid bet, as evidenced by the volume of company shares purchased at market value (think Disney, Coca-Cola, Proctor & Gamble, and Pfizer).

Next, goodwill and intangible assets appearing on the company's financial statements as a result of prior acquisitions are identified. We add these components to the unrecorded intangible assets previously calculated to yield the value of total intellectual capital. As an example, in the case of Proctor & Gamble, the value of the brands Gillette (acquisition) and Tide (unrecorded) are in effect being added together as part of total intellectual capital.

Intellectual capital is entirely the result of talent, as is demonstrated in forthcoming chapters. The important thing to note is that the value of IC includes the value the market places on an entity's human capital and can be accurately and objectively calculated for publicly traded companies (and with the right data, for nonpublic companies as well).

To summarize, the following algorithm is used to calculate what is deemed the intellectual capital index (ICI) for a company:

Book Value:

Shareholder's Equity + Net Debt (that is, Debt – Cash and Marketable Securities)

Enterprise Value:

[Market Share Price × Shares Issued and Outstanding] + Net Debt

Intellectual Capital:

Intangible Assets (on books) + Goodwill + [Enterprise Value-Book Value]

Intellectual Capital Index (ICI):

Intellectual Capital ÷ Enterprise Value

Intellectual capital, as you will soon see, accounts for roughly 80% of the value of the average public corporation today. What is the "means of production" for the majority of this enterprise value? People and their human capital. Yes, people are literally, not just figuratively, the most important asset of many companies across many industries in today's knowledge-driven economy.

This logic of connecting people with value should, once and for all, cast aside the notion that referring to employees as "assets" or "human capital" is derogatory or demeaning. In fact, it's just the opposite and, only when recognized as such, can organizations truly leverage talent in the way they have historically leveraged other valuable assets.

Endnotes

1. According to U.S. Generally Accepted Accounting Principles (GAAP), including FAS 13.

2. The Future of Accounting and Financial Reporting, Steven M.H. Wallman, AICPA Twenty-third National Conference on Current SEC Reporting.

3

Valuing and Evaluating Companies and Their Intellectual Capital

- *Determining a company's market value*
- *What is the difference between labor and human capital?*
- *The Intellectual Capital Index (ICI) applied*
- *How and why does intellectual capital vary by industry?*

There are entire volumes written solely on the subject of valuing companies, but to greatly simplify a complex topic, company valuations are based on the discounted value of expected future cash flows. Every analyst following a company maintains a cash flow model that is constantly updated for news that will materially affect both the company's valuation and advice given to investors regarding the fair value of the company's shares (and prospective fair value). Those future cash flows, in turn, are driven by the performance of a company's assets (see Figure 3.1). As such, although anticipated cash flow is used to calculate a company's market value, that value is ultimately attributed directly to the underlying assets—both tangible and intangible—as evidenced by *business combination accounting*.

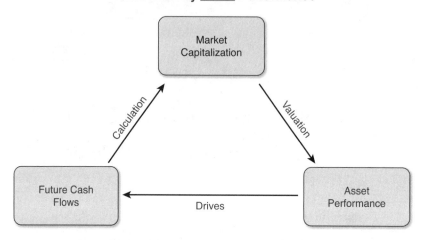

**Business Value Is Based on Future Cash
Flow Driven by <u>Asset</u> Performance**

Figure 3.1 Business Valuation

© 2014 Human Capital Formation, LLC

Figure 3.2 depicts this allocation of asset value to both tangible and intangible assets. As described in the previous chapter, although there are other categories of intangible assets, intellectual capital is the focus of this book because of its strategic connection to the human capital provided by an organization's talent. It is the category that drives the greatest market value in most companies today. Human capital is the only "active" subcategory in intellectual capital and is the source of all other IC subcategories, which are "inert." (This is discussed at length in the next chapter.) Also, I've defined human capital as the productive capacity of "knowledge workers," a part of the employed workforce. Human capital is the means of production for intellectual capital. As you will see, the value split between tangible and intangible assets depends on a number of factors, most importantly the type of industry a business operates in.

Two Different Types Of Assets

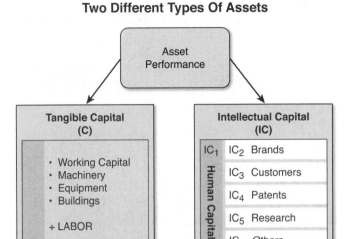

Figure 3.2 Tangible and Intellectual Capital Components
© 2014 Human Capital Formation, LLC

Linda: How does "labor" on the tangible capital section of your chart differ from "human capital" on the intellectual capital side of your chart?

Tom: With tangible capital, the investment is actually made in assets such as machinery and equipment. Labor, for example a machine operator, is an expense that is input to activate the machine and enable it to be productive. When it comes to intellectual capital, the investment is made in human capital. Human capital is the asset that produces intellectual capital as an output. Human capital is the "means of production."

A pure example of this is the biotechnology industry where scientists are the key assets; without scientists, the firm would own no intellectual property in the form of patents or licenses and would have no products. The capital investment in a new bio-technology firm initially funds the acquisition of scientists and their output.[1]

Linda: Human capital is definitely an asset that companies invest in—but it's not included on financial statements due to accounting rules? I always see "Salaries" as the primary expense on my P&L.

Tom: That's correct, which explains a large part of the disparity between market values and book values of public corporations. The human capital asset cannot be included on financial statements. You do see the current expense for people in "Salaries" and "Cost of Goods Sold," but no asset.

There are other obvious characteristics that distinguish labor from human capital; labor is physical, and human capital is intangible. Although labor and human capital are both capabilities of people, those capabilities play different roles in the economic model and capitalization of a firm.

Linda: So, are you saying that all jobs are either labor or human capital-oriented?

Tom: Many jobs are either predominantly labor or predominantly human capital-oriented. But there is a great "in-between" that is growing. Manufacturing labor increasingly requires skills to operate advanced technology, and much of the remaining labor pool has evolved into service occupations that use technology as well. However, the main roles that produce intellectual capital and drive market values in today's knowledge-driven economy are clearly human capital-oriented.

Using the ICI algorithm from the preceding chapter, companies can be analyzed to determine the proportion of intellectual capital value to their total enterprise value. Why is this important? For a number of reasons, including:

- It provides an objective measure of, and a means to focus on, the value of intellectual capital relative to total market value— the majority of value in the average modern corporation. It puts into perspective dependence on tangible versus intangible assets and informs priorities.

- It implies that building a talent strategy based on this analysis and evaluating it over time is the most effective way to grow shareholder value for the majority of companies.

- Comparing a company's IC analysis with that of competitors' provides strategic insight into value creation gaps and opportunities.

Figure 3.3 summarizes the results of applying the ICI algorithm to a representative sample of Fortune 500 companies covering a variety of industries.

As you can see, the table is sorted in order by ICI from highest to lowest. A higher or lower ICI does not mean one company is necessarily more successful or valuable than another, particularly when they are not in the same industry. What a high IC% would indicate is a higher dependence on talent for sustaining and growing market value relative to other organizations.

2012 Reported Year-End Values ($ billions)							
Company	Fortune Rank 2013	Enterprise Value (EV)	Book Value	Estimated Value of Intellectual Capital (IC)			Intellectual Capital Index (ICI)
				On-Books	Off-Books	Total IC	(Total IC÷EV)
P & G	28	$237	$94	$87	$142	$229	97%
Amazon	49	$114	$8	$2	$106	$108	95%
Amgen	162	$99	$35	$28	$64	$92	93%
Microsoft	35	$249	$41	$18	$209	$226	91%
UPS	53	$75	$10	$3	$65	$68	91%
eBay	196	$61	$16	$10	$45	$55	89%
Merck	58	$151	$60	$41	$91	$132	88%
Conagra	209	$24	$15	$12	$9	$21	88%
Coca-Cola	57	$178	$49	$19	$128	$148	84%
3M	101	$65	$20	$9	$46	$55	84%
Walmart	1	$275	$125	$21	$150	$171	62%
Walgreens	37	$48	$22	$4	$26	$30	61%
Deere	85	$72	$33	$1	$39	$40	55%
Weyerhaeuser	363	$18	$8	-	$10	$10	55%
Target	36	$53	$30	-	$23	$23	43%
Archer Daniels	27	$27	$27	$.6	$.04	$.6	2%

Figure 3.3 ICI Calculations for Selected Companies

Note: Data sources are respective company annual reports, year-end stock values, and proprietary calculations.

© 2014 Human Capital Formation, LLC

Linda: Wouldn't a company with a higher ICI probably be a better bet for investors in the long-term?

Tom: Maybe yes and maybe no. Investing of course is a balance between risk and reward. The returns on IC are very high, but in many cases the risks are as well. An interesting accounting research study published in *The Accounting Review* and involving hundreds of companies concluded that, on average, $1 invested in R&D leads to a $5 increase in market value over a seven-year period of time. The growth in the value of the average company over the past decades has been mostly attributable to intangible value, as has the growth in the Dow Jones Industrial Average, so these are arguments for leaning in the IC direction. At the same time, as you can see by the table in Figure 3.3, many different industries have significant IC value and opportunity for growth. Investing wisely involves understanding lots of variables and considerations other than the relative size of IC. What I would say, however, is a company that expects to grow its value via IC over the long haul will be dependent on the quality of talent it has and its ability to realize their contributions. As an investor, I would look closely at that company's prospects for doing those things as an investment prerequisite.

Insights and Considerations from an Analysis of Select Companies

The analysis of data such as that included in Figure 3.3 will yield an abundance of insight and information about companies and industries. A number of key insights about the specific companies included here and observations about industries and the calculation itself are laid out in the following sections.

Size Doesn't Matter

It is notable that the Fortune 500 ranking is by size of revenue, which has little bearing on the percentage of intellectual capital value to total value. Walmart is #1 on the Fortune 500 list while Proctor & Gamble is #28 but ranked highest on the table in Figure 3.3 in terms of IC% of value. Archer Daniels Midland is #27 (larger than P&G) on the Fortune 500 but at the bottom of the ICI ranking in the table.

It is also instructive to note that the highest ICI industries tend to be consumer products, technology, and pharmaceuticals. But there are some surprises—among them, UPS, Walmart, and Conagra, which are all valued more for their intellectual capital than their tangible assets.

UPS

UPS, known as the largest shipment and logistics company in the world, has over 6 million customers and nearly 400,000 employees around the globe. Considering all the tangible assets one would imagine UPS has (distribution centers, trucks, airplanes, and so on), it would make sense to assume that the company has a lower ICI than most. Yet, when one analyzes their intellectual capital, UPS looks more like a technology company. A peek under the UPS hood shows a business built on a foundation of knowledge more than any other asset.

So although it is true that UPS has built and maintains a tangible global service delivery pipeline, it is powered by proprietary, integrated information systems, and increasingly, by deep knowledge in industries where it offers unique and high margin services, such as in pharmaceuticals. UPS offers value-added services in shipping and storage accompanied by requisite regulatory knowledge that make it the supply chain partner of choice for other high-end, rapidly expanding global industries.

All of these capabilities are reflected in a UPS market valuation that is 16 times its book value, compared to an industry average of 3.5 and S&P of 4.6.[2]

Walmart

Walmart, a bricks and mortar giant and the largest company in the Fortune 500 based on revenue, has over 11,000 locations and 2.2 million employees. Yet 62% of the value of the company lies in intellectual capital. Within the industry, the retailer is famous as a logistics and supply chain juggernaut; their intellectual capital in this arena is legendary and nearly priceless. When I was CFO at Revlon, Walmart was our largest customer by far.

Two things strike me about Walmart when reflecting on my experiences with them: 1) their requirements of suppliers were very tough and very strict (we had to bend over backward to serve them); 2) because they themselves were so disciplined and efficient (relative to other customers), we had high profit margins on their business, so it was worth our time and resources to bend over backward for them. Based on analysis, Walmart is another example of a business with a great deal invested in hard assets—buildings, inventory, vehicles, and so on—yet investors purchase shares at market value more for their intellectual capital than any of that.

Conagra

Conagra is in fact a consumer products company, but it wasn't always that way. Conagra began in 1919 as the Nebraska Consolidated Mills Company. After a few early attempts to move up the value stream (they invented and then sold Duncan Hines in the 1950s), the 1980s saw consumer product additions to the Conagra family that included Banquet Foods Co., Armour Food Co., Del Monte frozen food business, and the launch of Healthy Choice branded dinners. By the early 1990s, Conagra had an intellectual capital percentage of 70, just south of the pure consumer products companies.

Today, Conagra is squarely positioned in the consumer products landscape and has an ICI of 88%. Imagine the shift of talent that took place during the late 1990s and 2000s as that enterprise rapidly and significantly evolved. Today, Conagra has a large portfolio of successful brands including Orville Redenbacher's, Chef Boyardee, Hunt's, Hebrew National, Peter Pan, and Egg Beaters, among many others.

IC: On or Off the Books?

Proctor & Gamble is a great example of a company that has significant intellectual capital both on the books and off the books. The following is an overview of the circumstances that drive each of those situations at the company. This overview will also serve to help understand similar situations at many other companies.

P&G's $53 billion acquisition of Gillette in 2005 offers a great example of when a company is permitted, in fact required, to record the value of intangible assets on its books (see Figure 3.4). Essentially all of the net asset value recognized in this purchase was attributed to intangible assets and goodwill. How is it possible that a global company like Gillette, with 31 manufacturing operations in 14 countries around the world, is comprised of assets that are more than 85% intangible? What about all that brick and mortar? It is worth noting that accounting rules do require that tangible assets are valued in an acquisition at fair market value, so there isn't a lot of room for lowballing there.

The reality is that after 104 years and the accumulated output of countless thousands of "knowledge workers," Gillette's huge trove of intellectual capital was driving all the cash flow and accounted for most of its value. It is that simple.

The following table presents the preliminary allocation of purchase price related to the Gillette business as of the date of the acquisition.	
Current assets	$ 5,553
Property, plant and equipment	3,673
Goodwill	34,943
Intangible assets	29,736
Other noncurrent assets	771
TOTAL ASSETS ACQUIRED	74,676
Current liabilities	5,009
Noncurrent liabilities	16,241
TOTAL LIABILITIES ASSUMED	21,250
NET ASSETS ACQUIRED	53,426

The Gillette acquisition resulted in $34.94 billion in goodwill, preliminarily allocated primarily to the segments comprising the Gillette businesses (Blades and Razors, Duracell and Braun, HealthCare and Beauty).

Figure 3.4 P&G Purchase Price Allocation of Gillette Business
Source: Proctor & Gamble 2006 Annual Report

Of the $87 billion of "on-books" intellectual capital shown for P&G (refer to Figure 3.3), a whopping $65 billion originated with the Gillette acquisition. The excerpts shown here from the P&G 2006 Annual Report shed more light on how these assets are recorded in an acquisition. The acquired "intangibles" break down into two accounting classifications, goodwill and intangible assets, each of which I briefly describe.

Intangible assets valued in this acquisition totaled $29.7 billion (see Figure 3.5). Intangible assets in this accounting classification must be separately identifiable. The brands Gillette, Duracell, and Oral-B are good examples. Also, specific technologies and customer agreements and relationships are often separately identifiable. The second category, goodwill, represents other intangible value that is not deemed to be "separable" and specifically includes value assigned to the acquired workforce. Goodwill was valued at nearly $35 billion in the Gillette acquisition. As you can imagine, in addition to developed brands and intellectual capital that are already part of operations, a great deal of research and knowledge that is not necessarily "separable" exists at any point in time and can be among the most valuable of assets in driving future cash flow. All of this value is, in effect, captured as goodwill in an acquisition. Intangibles and goodwill are tested and evaluated annually to reaffirm or adjust their future value as carried on the books.

The preliminary purchase price allocation to the identifiable intangible assets included in these financial statements is as follows:		
		Weighted Average Life
INTANGIBLE ASSETS WITH DETERMINABLE LIVES		
Brands	$ 1,607	20
Patents and technology	2,716	17
Customer relationships	1,445	27
BRANDS WITH INDEFINITE LIVES	23,968	Indefinite
TOTAL INTANGIBLE ASSETS	29,736	

Figure 3.5 P&G Intangible Asset Price Allocation—Gillette Acquisition
Source: Proctor & Gamble 2006 Annual Report

The "off-books" portion of intellectual capital (see Figure 3.3) is the portion that current accounting rules do not allow to be recorded as assets on the financial statements. So for P&G, that means that Tide, Crest, Bounty, and a very long list of other brands and intangible assets (including an assembled workforce of over 100,000!). All of this immense value is not recorded in the company's financial statements. We calculate the off-books value as the difference between enterprise value (what shareholders pay) and book value (what the books say).

Finally, to determine the total value of intellectual capital, we add IC on the books (say, from acquisitions) to what we calculate as the off-books amount. In the case of P&G, this results in a whopping 97% of enterprise value.

IC Varies by Industry Characteristics

It is pretty intuitive that technology companies such as Amazon, Microsoft, and eBay would have most of their value wrapped up in intellectual capital. Merck's value, and pharmaceuticals in general, is also driven by intellectual capital. Merck's 2012 10-K reflected more than two-dozen active patents for key products in the marketplace, many more products at different stages of development and regulatory clearance, and 13,600 employees and $8.6 billion dedicated to research and development. Therefore, it's easy to understand why 88% of Merck's value is intellectual capital.

In most industries, even heavily tangible asset-laden businesses, the market leaders have much of their value recognized as intellectual capital. Market leaders typically have a proprietary edge with customers and will often own the best practice methods within their industries. In addition, you can expect to see a scale advantage, strong branding, and other valuable intangible assets.

On the flipside, commodity businesses do not survive on intellectual capital. Archer-Daniels-Midland Company is one of the world's largest processors of oilseeds, corn, wheat, cocoa, and other agricultural commodities. ADM's 2012 sales revenue was higher than P&G, Microsoft, and Merck, coming in at #27 of the Fortune 500. This is a high volume, low margin industry. Efficiency in capital, cost, and cash management is the essential driver. And without a doubt, this is a solid, well-run business. However, it is not an industry and business model that is designed to create intellectual capital as a means of generating shareholder value.

In fiscal 2012, Archer-Daniels-Midland Company recorded sales revenue of about $89 billion versus $47 billion for Merck & Company. ADM invested $28 million in R&D, while Merck invested $8.6 billion in the same time period. These are very different industries with different reliance on intellectual capital for their success. Eighty-eight percent of Merck's enterprise value is attributable to intellectual capital; ADM's is about 2% based on 2012 financial information.

Using the ICI to Analyze Companies Within Industries

One of the most valuable and relevant aspects of this information is the ability to compare players within the same industry. It is useful to look at Walmart and Target as an example. Walmart, as the largest retailer in the world, tops the Fortune 500 chart in sales revenue. Target has historically been a strong competitor in the mass market retail industry, cleverly honing an image that positioned them as the preferred choice for the middle to upper-middle class consumer, while Walmart appealed to a more rural and blue collar customer base. In the prerecession year ending January 2006, applying the ICI algorithm to Walmart yields a result of 69%, and for Target Corporation, 60%. Different strategies, different brand positions, but the same industry, with strong results and comparable value from their IC for shareholders. Fast-forward to 2012, and Figure 3.3 shows that Walmart has more or less maintained the relative value of its intellectual capital at 62%, but Target has suffered significant depletion to only 43% (as of the fiscal 2013 year end, the ICI remained at 62% for Walmart and dropped to 40% for Target).

What caused Target's precipitous decline in less than ten years? Interestingly, the CEO's forced resignation in May 2014 provides us some clues. On the surface, his departure was connected to the widely publicized consumer data breach late in 2013, but there was undoubtedly more to it than that. There had been ongoing concern among analysts and the media regarding Target's business strategy and the belief in some circles that the corporation had lost its way. Target took heat for what some perceived as an ineffective expansion into Canada and was criticized for merchandising that seems to turn away from its core customer. This information lends itself to the market's recognition of a decline in intellectual capital value for Target over the last ten years.

In later chapters I discuss how to dive into the detail of intellectual capital value and influence its direction through organization change and strategic decisions. Utilizing available public information, the techniques for diving deeper can also assist in better understanding competitors and gaining insight on opportunities that exist to improve your relative position.

Linda: If I see that I'm lagging in IC% value when compared to others in my industry, what exactly does that mean? And what can I do about it?

Tom: Without further analysis, the difference with competitors simply means that investors expect IC of those other firms to have relatively more impact on driving cash flow than yours. They are recognizing the intangible advantage of competitors by the price they pay for their stock. This is normally true in the case of the industry leader, for example...as long as they are poised to continue leading.

Analysis of the difference between you and competitors identifies areas of opportunity and can redirect strategic decisions, particularly with respect to talent. What are the main components of a competitor's IC? Where are your gaps? What are your choices? Because human capital uniquely produces IC, the talent implications have to be identified and talent investment disproportionately channeled to address them.

Using the ICI to Analyze Individual Companies over Time

Another interesting way to gain insight from IC value analysis is to track a particular company's movement over time. We got a glimpse of this when we looked at the movement of Target in comparison with Walmart. The Coca-Cola Company is also an interesting example to view over time. In Figure 3.3, Coke's tally is an ICI of about 84%, reflecting world famous brands including its namesake as well as Sprite and Fanta, in addition to a multitude of other forms of intellectual capital (unique franchise system, global reach, strategic customer partnerships, and so on). However, this percentage has been somewhat diluted compared to the calculation prior to purchasing the North America bottling business from Coca-Cola Enterprises (CCE) in 2010. CCE, being a tangible, asset-intensive business, had the impact of lowering the relative percentage of intellectual capital value to total enterprise value for Coca-Cola. In 2009 (before the acquisition), Coke's ICI was 89%. Again, this result isn't necessarily good or bad but, in the long run, it paints a different picture from an investor's standpoint in terms of how the enterprise value grows and at what rate. In the case of Coke, acquiring and selling bottling operations is a method of continuously evolving and upgrading the entire system, so you would expect this impact to be temporary.

Sourcing Data Used in the ICI Calculation

For readers interested in understanding or applying this method to their own research, this section focuses on how to perform an analysis of intellectual capital value for public companies and offers some suggestions for achieving the same for privately-held enterprises.

The primary source of information for this analysis of public companies is the annual report on Form 10-K, which is required of public companies by the U.S. Securities and Exchange Commission (SEC). The 10-K is due to be filed within 60 days following the company's year-end for large companies (> $700 million of public float) and up to 90 days for smaller filers. Most companies choose a calendar year-end, but many choose a fiscal year ending in a month other than December, usually due to industry seasonal considerations. The 10-K provides a comprehensive overview of the company's business and financial condition and includes a full set of audited financial statements.

As you'll remember from Chapter 2, "Is Your Most Important Asset Really an Asset?," the ICI algorithm is

Book Value:

Shareholder's Equity + Net Debt (that is, Debt – Cash and Marketable Securities)

Enterprise Value:

[Market Share Price × Shares Issued and Outstanding] + Net Debt

Intellectual Capital:

Intangible Assets (on books) + Goodwill + [Enterprise Value-Book Value]

Intellectual Capital Index (ICI):

Intellectual Capital ÷ Enterprise Value

Figure 3.6 lays out the section of the 10-K where each data element used in the algorithm is typically found (or cites another source). Normally, only the closing stock price comes from a source other than the 10-K. In most cases, the 10-K discloses stock prices on an average basis over a period of time; we are calculating the IC value at the balance sheet date, which is the reason we seek a specific closing price.

The names for the "data elements" mentioned in the table are not always consistent across different companies' 10-Ks, and there is some leeway with the SEC in naming conventions, so names similar to those in the table may be found instead. Also, the list in the table is not exhaustive for the different types of debt instruments and "near cash" names that might exist.

Calculation	Component	Data Elements	Source
Book Value	Shareholder's Equity	Shareholder's Equity	Balance Sheet-10K
	Net Debt	Notes Payable	Balance Sheet-10K
		Loans Payable	Balance Sheet-10K
		Current Maturities of Long Term Debt	Balance Sheet-10K
		Long Term Debt	Balance Sheet-10K
		Cash and Cash Equivalents	Balance Sheet-10K
		Short Term Investments	Balance Sheet-10K
		Marketable Securities	Balance Sheet-10K
Enterprise Value	Stock Price	Closing Price on date of balance sheet	Yahoo Finance or similar
	# Shares	Shares Issued and Outstanding (i.e. net of Treasury Shares)	Balance Sheet or Statement of Shareowner's Equity-10k
Intellectual Capital	On Books	Trademarks	Balance Sheet-10K
		Intangible Assets	Balance Sheet-10K
		Goodwill	Balance Sheet-10K
	Off Books	Enterprise Value less Book Value	Calculation

Figure 3.6 Data Sources for ICI Calculation
© 2014 Human Capital Formation, LLC

The objective is to calculate an accurate "off-books" intellectual capital value by determining the difference between the amount at which the market is valuing a company on a debt-free basis (enterprise value) and the amount at which the books record the value, also on a debt-free basis (book value). Netting cash and "near cash" against the value of debt instruments provides a truer picture of actual debt than showing it on a gross basis. Obviously, adding the "off-books" and "on-books" values together give a solid and objective approximation of intellectual capital value.

What if the company is not a public company? How can one go about calculating the value of intellectual capital without a 10-K? The missing data will be the market valuation of the company. Many private companies have a working estimate of market value from a variety of sources ranging from some form of third-party valuation for a potential acquisition/sale transaction to a valuation in conjunction with securing bank or other type of capital financing. In the absence of an existing valuation estimate, a comparable company analysis (CCA) can be performed. Beyond the scope of this book, a CCA would involve finding the best comparable public company in the same industry and comparing key financial and other business data to provide for approximating the right market valuation.

The Potential Impact of Long-Lived Assets on the ICI Calculation

In the past, when attempting to explain the difference between market values and book values, some have speculated that the accounting for long-lived assets may be a key factor. Walmart and other large retailers, as an example, have a tremendous amount of buildings and real estate as part of their tangible assets, and these are all recorded at historic cost less depreciation in their published financial statements. It is possible, given current accounting standards, that some long-lived asset categories could be effectively undervalued on the balance sheet and understate reported tangible asset values. If that were the case, investors might pay more than book value for a stock not only because of IC, but also because they would place a higher than book value on the hard assets of these companies. The effect would be to lower the ICI shown in our calculations. Although that possibility exists, the following analysis provides evidence that the impact is not likely to be material in most cases.

The size and scale of Proctor & Gamble's acquisition of Gillette in 2005 provided a good opportunity to evaluate this concern. In that $53 billion acquisition, there was no material difference in historic property plant and equipment values and the fair value assigned to those assets by the purchaser at the time of the acquisition. Gillette had reported a net property, plant, and equipment value of $3.657 billion in their March 2005 10-Q, and Proctor & Gamble assigned $3.673 billion of the purchase price as the fair value of those assets in October 2005 (see Figure 3.4).

Overall, especially comparing within industries (which, arguably, is the most important application of the information), it is reasonable to expect that the valuation of long-lived assets in the financial statements will not materially alter the conclusions and direction provided by the ICI calculation and analysis.

Navigating Industry Oddities that Impact the ICI Calculation

In some instances, the ICI algorithm is imperfect. When looking at the range of industries in the public domain, there are a few that do not lend themselves well to this calculation without some adjustment. Here we discuss adjustments to the calculation for banking, insurance, investment and energy firms, as well as the reasons that make them necessary.

Financial services firms (banking, insurance, investment banking, and so on) are prominent in the Fortune 500 and in indices such as the Dow Jones Industrial Average, and adjustment to the IC calculation for these firms is necessary. Because of the business that banks are engaged in, the calculation of net debt (which impacts both book and enterprise values) has to be handled differently. Banks are in the business of borrowing and lending, and so the cash and debt (net debt) carried on their books are in large part more components of their working capital than a means of capitalizing the business. Banks are regulated in this regard and are required to maintain specific capital and debt ratios. As a result, we chose to limit our net debt components for banks to just the portion classified as long-term, with no offset for cash held on the balance sheet. This seems fair (but admittedly arbitrary) and should come close to an "apples to apples" comparison for the banking industry relative to other industries. In addition, this approach should allow banks themselves to be fairly comparable for ICI purposes. Some large corporations require like consideration if they have significant financing operations embedded in their consolidated balance sheets, such as with GE Capital.

Similar circumstances hold true for insurance and investment firms. When the items to be adjusted are not readily apparent from the details in financial reports, it makes more sense to simply use the difference between market value and book value of equity in the calculations rather than attempting to gross them up for net debt.

Last, due to the accounting rules for oil and gas reserves, energy companies such as Exxon Mobil and Chevron are the largest exceptions to the ICI algorithm. Although these reserves are the largest asset owned by these companies, accounting rules do not allow the reserves to be recorded on the books as an asset due to the uncertainty regarding their actual size and cost of recovery—and therefore value. They are, however, required to disclose extensive information regarding reserves in notes on the financial statements. Clearly, investors factor an estimate of the reserves value into the price they pay for the companies' stock, so when simply taking the difference between enterprise and book values, the value of oil reserves are picked up in addition to intellectual capital for these companies. To get a reasonable approximation of IC (considering the engineering and other expertise of these companies is substantial) the estimated value of the stated oil and gas reserves should be backed out of enterprise value as an adjustment before doing the calculation.

Endnotes

1. Julia Porter Liebeskind, "The New Relationship: Human Capital in the American Corporation," The Brookings Institution, 2000.

2. Zack's Investment Research, October 6, 2014.

4

Understanding Active and Inert Components of Intellectual Capital

- *How is intellectual capital created and accumulated?*
- *How is human capital organized to produce other intellectual capital?*
- *How can specific components of intellectual capital be identified?*

We know that intellectual capital is a category of intangible assets. Intellectual capital comprises the majority of value in most public corporations, as demonstrated earlier by the ICI algorithm and other financial information.

But what has caused the rapid expansion of intellectual capital value over the last 35 years, and what does its future growth depend on? The answer is its single active component—human capital.

The exponential growth of intellectual capital value in recent decades has been fueled by a longer-term investment in human capital that began accelerating in the first half of the 1900s in the U.S. Between 1940 and 1980, the number of college graduates increased ten-fold, representing many billions of dollars of investment in higher education. During that time period, colleges and universities in the U.S. transformed from being more an option for the socioeconomic elite to an alternative for a much wider demographic. Adding formal learning and skill building to cognitive ability en mass stoked the production of intellectual capital. This trend continued, evolved, and eventually became more focused on business-relevant human capital development.

The result is company market capitalizations that often reflect more than 80% intellectual capital value.

An organization's intellectual capital is, in effect, designed with the potential to proliferate. It necessarily includes both active and inert components (see Figure 4.1). The active component—human capital—happens in real time and produces ideas that generate an outflow of intangible property that can be bought or sold by its owner. That intangible property (which is inert intellectual capital) includes high value assets such as brands, patents, and commercial relationships.

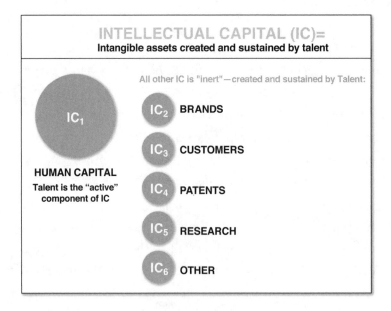

Figure 4.1 Active and Inert Intellectual Capital

© 2014 Human Capital Formation, LLC

Although people themselves cannot be bought or sold (in the absence of slavery), they can assign the rights to their human capital and its output. For example, employment and confidentiality agreements may allow people to convey to employers all their rights to any inventions, discoveries, and authorship made during their tenure and prohibit them from disclosing significant "work in progress" following the end of their employment. This makes sense in that human capital must be managed to optimize output.

As already noted, the output of human capital is intellectual capital, which exists in many forms including brands, patents, copyrights, trademarks, inventions, discoveries, methods, techniques, processes, relationships, and so on. However, all of these outputs are inert: They may have great value but are inanimate. Without talent actively managing them, they lose value until they become obsolete.

Inert intellectual capital requires input from human capital to stay relevant, to evolve, and to meet the changing needs of customers. When successfully managed, intellectual capital accumulates over time and can grow to become enormously valuable in a business—like brand Coca-Cola with an estimated value of $79 billion accumulated over 127 years. Intellectual capital (like a brand) can be accumulated *or depleted* over time, depending on the size and success of human capital and other related investments.

No doubt the accumulation of value in the brand Coke was not a straight line, and it is a safe bet that in some years along the way its value dipped. To illustrate this point, the brand's advertising slogans in the chart in Figure 4.2 give insight into how messaging evolved to support the brand's key strategic goals. These slogans reflect an attempt to connect with consumers of the time, and a few were unequivocal misses. In all cases, however, human capital was directed at the challenge of creating a slogan that would resonate with consumers at a given time and, overall, did so with tremendous success.

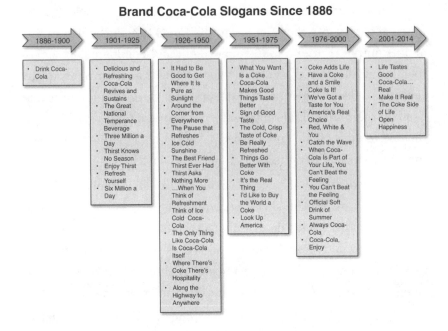

Figure 4.2 Evolution of Advertising for Brand Coca-Cola

Source: The Coca-Cola Company, www.coca-colacompany.com

Throughout the brand's history, thousands of smart marketers have been hired, organized, managed, and incented to understand what is relevant to consumers. This collective expertise, ingenuity and hard-work amassed knowledge and insights about consumers that propelled the messaging evolution from a simple request ("Drink Coca-Cola") to an emotional connection ("Open Happiness"). Ultimately, the results are clear: Key business metrics indicate how successfully their efforts matched consumer desires and, thus, advanced the brand.

Linda: What would provide a company with the biggest bang for their buck initially—improving the hiring of people into mission critical roles or retaining the people already in the roles?

Tom: It depends on the circumstances. Assuming you hire people into mission critical roles on an ongoing basis and retention is not a burning issue, I would focus on the hiring aspect.

In hiring for mission critical roles, you have to be able to optimize for quality of hire. In order to do this, you must take other variables that may compromise the quality objective, like hiring speed or diversity, off the table. You take those variables off the table by working ahead of the curve to build talent pipelines. Working ahead of the hiring need neutralizes the compromise of quality for speed and also affords the ability to develop a pipeline that meets diversity objectives. The investment in pipeline building solves the cost of compromise on the acquisition of mission critical talent.

On the other hand, if turnover in those mission critical roles were unusual, you would want the top priority to be gaining an understanding of the reasons for it. In general, understanding turnover (regardless of whether it is too high or too low) is one of the biggest missed opportunities for many companies. Some of the most revealing information spanning the entire employment life cycle can be derived from probing and analyzing turnover data.

It is important to recognize that hiring or retaining people in mission critical roles is not the issue; hiring and retaining *high quality* people in those roles is.

The Coca-Cola example is a familiar one that easily illustrates the idea of accumulating inert asset value through the efforts of active human capital over a long period of time. What better example of the accumulated brainpower of marketers and other experts could be imagined than the growth of a small, single-location, Atlanta-based pharmacy in 1886 to the global marketing, branding, and supply chain powerhouse that we know today?

Active Versus Inert

What is active, and what is inert in the Coca-Cola story? Although the slogans on the timeline are only a reflection of the research and thinking behind them, some were more effective than others. The results achieved provided new insights for the company's next generation of marketers charged with advancing the brand's value. This cycle in turn begat more research and innovation, more successes (and some failures), and continuous learning. The brand itself simply went up or down in value depending on the effectiveness of the human capital applied to it. The inert brand ("Coca-Cola") has always been dependent on the active human capital. Left alone, milked for cash or mismanaged, even the strongest brands will ultimately fail (Hummer, Atari, Polaroid, Borders Books, for example).

Of course this Coke story is an over-simplified depiction of building a brand; there is a lot more involved in brand-building than creating slogans. The point is: Value accumulates over time in the form of inert intellectual capital as a result of successfully deploying its active component—human capital—against a good idea (also produced by human capital!) Figure 4.3 depicts an example of how human capital (IC_1) is deployed to create, sustain, and grow a brand (IC_2). All inert intellectual capital is created in a similar fashion whether the IC is a brand, patent, technology, formula, or so on.

"Active" Human Capital Creates "Inert" IC Such As Brands

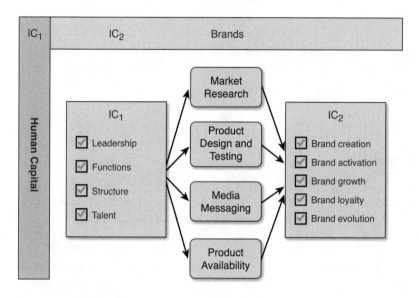

Figure 4.3 Creating Inert Intellectual Capital

© 2014 Human Capital Formation, LLC

The knowledge and skills that comprise human capital must be organized to be effective. This is what Peter Drucker referred to as "knowledge applied to knowledge." In a knowledge economy, leaders are knowledge workers themselves, whose expertise is in managing the application and performance of knowledge.

As such, Human Capital (IC_1) includes not only the talent with subject matter expertise, but also the leaders with strategic and operational expertise. Leadership provides the appropriate organizing mechanisms (for example, business units, functions, and so on) and work processes that orchestrate the output of talent efforts into a form that makes them effective.

In the case of a brand, human capital is channeled to work processes that ensure the appropriate market intelligence is gathered and understood, and that products are designed, made available, and promoted. Through this orchestration of efforts, human capital produces intellectual capital value that is owned by the firm.

> **Linda:** Once a company has identified a high-value-producing function within the organization, what should be done next to ensure that the opportunity for creating further value is maximized?
>
> **Tom:** Within those functions, which are determined via work processes that produce intellectual capital, critical roles are identified. Next, talent strategies exclusive to those roles must be developed that focus and direct the necessary investments (see Chapters 5, "Identifying Critical Roles Through Work Processes," and 6, "The New Talent Strategy Game Plan"). The way a business maximizes value is by concentrating investment on cash flow drivers. That is the whole point to identifying and investing in "critical roles"—to drive cash flow by investing in acquisition, development, and retention of the knowledge that produces intellectual capital.

The changes this new knowledge economy represents for leaders and managers cannot be overstated. Evolving from an era when the object of leadership was to enable the efficient deployment of land, labor, machinery, and equipment to one where leadership requires expertise in the deployment and performance of knowledge workers is a huge leap. Yet this is the leap that is required to propel organizations forward through the advantages that knowledge management offers. As the "founder of modern management," Peter Drucker said, "where there is effective management, that is, application of knowledge to knowledge, we can always obtain the other resources."[1] We delve further into this leadership aspect of "active" intellectual capital in Chapter 9, "Looking Back and Looking Forward," which deals with the work of critical talent and how to manage it.

But how can all of the important components of inert intellectual capital (and ultimately the human capital that produces it) that comprise a company's value be identified, especially from the outside? We did just that by examining Merck & Co., a global pharmaceutical and healthcare company.

The intellectual capital index algorithm tells us that Merck has an ICI of 88%, or total intellectual capital value of about $132 billion (refer to Figure 3.3, Chapter 3). By analyzing the narrative sections of Merck's 2013 Annual Report on Form 10-K, we can identify the significant components of their intellectual capital (see Figure 4.4). We will call our attempt illustrative, as the company itself—with a more complete understanding of their business levers—might take a different view.

IC Under the Microscope
Example: Merck & Co., Inc.*

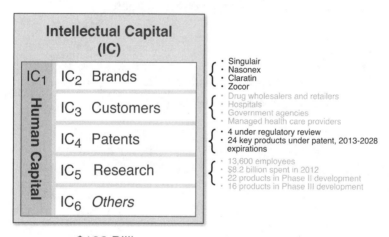

$132 Billion

Figure 4.4 Intellectual Capital Components Illustration

Note that about $41 billion of the IC was acquired through business combinations and is therefore on the books (refer to Figure 3.3, Chapter 3), while $91 billion is attributable to homegrown IC and not on the books following accounting rules as described in Chapter 3, "Valuing and Evaluating Companies and Their Intellectual Capital."

*Source: 2012 Merck & Co 10-K, selected illustrative data

© 2014 Human Capital Formation, LLC

Merck owns brands that are household names such as Singulair, Nasonex, Claratin, Zocor, and dozens more. The company also has a complex customer and distribution network, serving many market segments, that requires deep understanding and expertise.

The heart of any pharmaceutical company is research, resulting ultimately in patented products, following extensive and expensive phased development. Merck had $47 billion in sales along with a whopping $8.2 billion in research spending in 2012, contrasted with Proctor & Gamble, for example, which had $84 billion in sales and $2 billion in reported spending on R&D. Research and development is important to the consumer products industry in general, but in pharmaceuticals, its importance is unparalleled.

With a workforce of 13,600 dedicated to research, Merck's critical human capital is activated to maintain a current pipeline of 38 products in phase II and phase III development. It is therefore not difficult to understand why investors in effect attribute 88% of Merck's value to intellectual capital.

Linda: If intangible assets are so valuable, how is it possible that companies don't account for them, even just internally?

Tom: On the one hand, companies actually do a great job of describing intangible assets to investors—just look at any Investor Relations presentation—because those assets are such important drivers of cash flow, and hence share value. But they rarely indicate specific value for them.

The problem is, accounting requires accounting standards, and there aren't any for recording intangible assets that are developed internally, like brands. While investors place value on intellectual capital via the price they pay for stock, in the absence of standards, companies would end up establishing a myriad of ways to allocate the value among assets, creating inconsistent and therefore unreliable numbers. It's also a tricky proposition if you're a public company; the more information you create, the more you have to make public and track and disclose material changes.

Ultimately, because of the scale and growth of intellectual capital, I expect regulatory authorities (SEC, FASB, and so on) will find a way to address this accounting need, which is in the best interest of investors (discussed further in Chapter 9).

These are the significant categories of intellectual capital that are apparent for Merck based on their 10-K report. This intellectual property is poised to drive cash flow now and in the future via patented and pipeline products distributed through a multisegment distribution network. Again, most of this value is not on the books of Merck & Co. Looking from the outside in, we do not have a practical way of distributing the $132 billion value among those categories, but if we were inside the company, we would be able to devise reasonable estimates. And if we were purchasing the company, we would be compelled to do so.

The reasons, then, are clear as to why intellectual capital represents such a high percentage of enterprise value for most companies. Now that we understand the active component—human capital—and how inert intellectual capital is created, the building blocks are in place for developing strategies that accelerate market valuation through talent.

Endnote

1. Peter Drucker, Post-Capitalist Society, HarperBusiness, 1993

5

Identifying Critical Roles Through Work Processes

- *Creating a value-driven talent strategy*
- *How can intellectual capital be connected to critical roles?*
- *What is the best way to determine critical success factors?*

It is essential that before we drill down into identifying critical roles, we first understand the importance and recommended approach for building a value-driven talent strategy. After all, we've already learned how to calculate intellectual capital value (Chapter 3, "Valuing and Evaluating Companies and Their Intellectual Capital") in addition to how to identify its component parts (Chapter 4, "Understanding Active and Inert Components of Intellectual Capital"). This chapter marks the transition from the business strategy itself to the talent implications of the business strategy. From here, the talent strategy becomes the foundation for all human capital-related effort, activities, and outcomes that follow.

Building a value-driven talent strategy (VTS) is illustrated in Figure 5.1.

VALUE-DRIVEN TALENT STRATEGY

STAGE 1	STAGE 2	STAGE 3
Connecting talent strategy with value creation begins by understanding the relative importance and composition of intellectual capital within a company's valuation. Intellectual capital value can be calculated using the ICI algorithm (Chapter 2). Components can be identified by evaluating the make up of IC (Chapter 4).	Critical success factors, the things that must be done well, are prioritized by their importance to creating, sustaining, and growing intellectual capital. Priorities vary, especially by industry. Via the work processes associated with high priority CSFs, organization and roles are mapped and categorized.	Roles categorized as critical based on their importance to priority CSFs are set apart. All roles, critical and non-critical, are evaluated for their market availability. Roles are plotted on a four box matrix with axes for Criticality and Market Availability to enable systematic consideration of talent options and actions.

Figure 5.1 Framework: Value-Driven Talent Strategy

© 2014 Human Capital Formation, LLC

As you can see from the table, there are three stages to the value-driven talent strategy:

Stage 1

In Chapter 3, we discussed how to isolate and understand the value of intellectual capital, which is ultimately the object of our talent strategy.

Stage 2

In this chapter, a methodology is illustrated for identifying CSFs and associated work processes and mapping talent to the work.

Stage 3

In Chapter 6, "The New Talent Strategy Game Plan," we map out an approach for how to over-invest in the most value-driving talent within the organization.

Linda: It seems as if identifying value-creating roles might get complicated—with different leaders weighing in and debating about the relative value of different functions or roles. What's the best way to have these conversations in order to get the most accurate conclusions?

Tom: I think the best way for many companies to have these conversations is to begin by looking at what they already say to shareholders. Most companies have put the time and thought into conveying what things are really unique and special about themselves and what their points of competitive advantage are. In this story for shareholders you will find the major components of the firm's intellectual capital—the reasons shareholders should be confident about future cash flow.

Because attracting investors and protecting proprietary information is a balancing act, this information would likely have to be examined internally at a greater level of detail than that which is available to the public.

With that as a starting point, executives can then objectively look at the organization and recognize that there are certain functions and roles where the human capital in them is vital to the future cash flow story, and other roles that are simply important.

Again, the focus of this exercise is on the criticality of roles, not the people in them. That is an important concept to facilitate an objective assessment. It is entirely possible that high-potential talent is developed within roles that are not "critical" but become a talent pipeline for critical roles in the future. But to determine the roles critical to driving market value, it is important to separate the role's contribution from the talent.

Now that we share this common framework, how do we determine which are the most critical roles in any given firm? As I learned through experience so many years ago leading Finance for Coca-Cola in Germany, the way to identify these roles is to connect the desired output, in this case intellectual capital, with the work that produces it.

But what specific work results in a lucrative patent or a successful brand? The first step in Stage 2 is to identify what must be done well to achieve these IC goals; we call these *critical success factors* (CSF). Identifying CSFs is an essential step for two reasons:

- It provides a means to identify and focus on work that is truly critical.

- It prevents overlooking work that is essential but not apparently so.

Any CSF may have multiple work processes that contribute to delivering it, but a few will be higher priority based on their contribution and output. These higher priority work processes are where concentrations of critical roles are present. In a moment, you'll read an example that illustrates this concept.

Objectively identifying critical roles is the cornerstone to building a value-driven talent strategy. After critical roles are identified, decisions can be made regarding how to source, attract, select, and retain that talent.

Let's go back to brand Coca-Cola once again for a hypothetical example of workflow (see Figure 5.2) associated with a value-driven talent strategy. Afterward, we broaden this approach to a sample of various industries.

On December 31, 2012, the enterprise value of The Coca-Cola Company was approximately $178 billion. The value attributed to intellectual capital was approximately $148 billion or 84% of the total (see Figure 3.3, Chapter 3). We also know that Interbrand, a brand consulting firm, has separately estimated brand Coca-Cola to have a value of $79 billion, so for this hypothetical example we separate that component of IC from the total to illustrate our example.

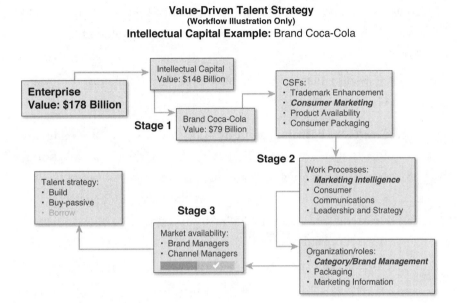

Value-Driven Talent Strategy
(Workflow Illustration Only)
Intellectual Capital Example: Brand Coca-Cola

Figure 5.2 Coke VTS Example
© 2014 Human Capital Formation, LLC

Remember—the objective of a value-driven talent strategy is to ensure the strategy is built around those assets that drive the greatest value (cash flow) for shareholders. Obviously, brand Coca-Cola is one of those assets. With that we have our simplified view of Stage 1.

In Stage 2, we are seeking to understand how that $79 billion brand value is produced—created, sustained, grown—to help us identify the most critical human capital. To do that, we connect the dots between critical success factors, work processes, and the organization and roles within it.

Critical Success Factors (CSF)

Companies must do many things well to be successful. A number of those things stand out as higher priorities for producing specific intellectual capital. Of all the things that must be done well at Coca-Cola, which are the most important to growing the value of the brand Coke?

Let's assume that the following four CSFs are the most important in our Coke brand example:

1. **Trademark Enhancement**—All of the things the company does that creates a positive impression for the Coca-Cola trademark. (Company and brand happen to share the same name!) These could be as far ranging as the company's sustainability initiatives and college scholarship program for high achieving high school students.

2. **Consumer Marketing**—Connecting with consumers and delivering against their needs better than the competition.

3. **Product Availability**—Wherever, whenever, and however the consumer wants it.

4. **Consumer Packaging**—The contour bottle, the up-to-date yet historic script, the color red.

From these four, let's select Consumer Marketing (#2) as the CSF to carry through to the next connection with work processes in this abbreviated illustration. (In practice of course, we would carry the other three priority CSFs through as well.)

Work Processes

What work processes must come together to achieve success for the CSF, Consumer Marketing?

Under examination, we might determine that Consumer Marketing is primarily delivered through the following work streams:

a. **Marketing Intelligence**—All of the work involved in understanding consumer and market behaviors.

b. **Consumer Communications**—The work involved in crafting and delivering effective consumer messages.

c. **Leadership and Strategy**—The work involved in leading, prioritizing, and communicating activity against this CSF (note that "Leadership and Strategy" is a priority work process for each CSF).

Again, in this abbreviated illustration, we select Marketing Intelligence (a) as the work process to carry through to the next connection with organization and roles.

Organization/Roles

After identifying Marketing Intelligence as the work process, it should be straightforward to connect the organization units and roles that perform that work.

Depending on size and complexity, many companies find that multiple organization units are involved in any given work process. In the case of the Marketing Intelligence work process, we may find organization units such as the following involved in doing the work:

- **Category/Brand Management**—Role is to define the marketing intelligence priorities, requirements, and objectives.

- **Packaging**—Role is to define specialized marketing intelligence requirements for consumer and market packaging studies.

- **Marketing Information**—Role is to design, conduct, and interpret consumer and market studies.

Finally, we would look into each of the organization units themselves to determine specific roles that should be deemed "critical." These are target rich organization units because they directly connect to the work that is critical to a significant part of IC and market value. When we complete the identification of critical roles, we are finished with Stage 2. Many—but not all—roles in these units will likely be considered critical; let's assume that brand managers and channel managers have been identified as critical roles in our example.

This Coke example has provided a simple illustration of the process for identifying critical success factors and connecting them with specific, essential roles.

In Stage 3, discussed in the next chapter, availability of these critical roles is determined, which will ultimately round out the analysis and lead to talent strategy decisions.

Linda: For a business with an ICI of 90% or more, doesn't determining critical roles become a never-ending exercise? Isn't almost every function in such a company driving value?

Tom: No, the percentage of IC really doesn't relate to how many critical roles an organization has or how many functions they sit in. This can be dramatically different from industry to industry and organization to organization. Proctor & Gamble, for example, with over 120,000 employees but 97% IC value, no doubt has many functions and roles that are important but not "critical" to driving that value. Google, on the other had, has 40% of its workforce in just R&D, so that is likely a different story.

What *is* true about a high percentage of IC is that the critical roles that do exist are of very high importance to driving the overall value of the company. For this reason, it is wise to identify them and ensure that the right investments are unfailingly made to preserve these assets. That is the significance of connecting the market value, through intellectual capital value, as directly as possible to the source.

But in practice, how does one identify the highest priority critical success factors to begin with?

We find that companies have often already articulated, at least internally, what comprises their highest priority critical success factors. In more than one company that we work with, these are referred to internally as "pillars." In any substantial business, if you were starting the analysis from scratch, it wouldn't be unusual to produce a long list of more than a dozen CSFs in total. Considering that businesses typically have customers, consumers, suppliers, investors, employees, and other stakeholders as well as multiple internal support functions, there are many things that must be done well for the business to be considered a success. Although most jobs exist for very good reasons, not all of them are critical roles in terms of producing intellectual capital and creating market value.

To determine which are critical, you simply have to take the long list of things that must be done well and prioritize (rate and rank) them against the intellectual capital that drives the business. Five or six CSFs will rise to the top, aligned with what the greatest value to the business is.

The objective of Stage 2 is to identify the roles that are most important to delivering critical success factors. As we saw in the Coke brand workflow illustration, in large and complex environments, connecting key work processes is an essential link to identifying these roles. Multiple organization units often contribute significantly to the execution of a single work process. In smaller, less complex entities, it may be possible to go directly to connecting organization units with critical success factors, eliminating the extra analysis of work processes, and achieving an accurate and complete identification of critical roles.

Now let's take a broader look at Stage 2 analysis for companies across multiple industries to better understand how connecting intellectual capital to CSFs leads to identifying the most critical roles.

Most companies, particularly public ones, have put a lot of effort (at least inadvertently) into pinpointing their principle intellectual capital and related critical success factors. Although often at a sweeping level, companies share information about assets and attributes, which they expect to have a positive impact on business and cash flow in the future. Because of SEC disclosure requirements (Regulation FD), any such information shared by public companies with investors, brokers or other stakeholders must be disclosed to the public.

As a result of these required disclosures, we get a good understanding of the most valuable intellectual capital and related critical success factors by reviewing public company documents and filings including the 10-K, 10-Q, Form 8-K, and Investor Relations presentations (often posted on company websites or filed on an 8-K). Internally, of course, you could expect access to a greater level of nonpublic detail regarding how a company intends to produce value (although not necessarily prioritized).

To further illustrate how Stage 2 of the value-driven talent strategy works, we used public information to create a view of intellectual capital components and related critical success factors for three well-known companies.

Figure 5.3 depicts an analysis of the information published by 3M, Walgreen Co., and UPS—three very successful companies in very different industries. Using this information as a starting point, our method of identifying critical roles is applied to each.

Understanding IC and Critical Success Factors

Company	Industry	Intellectual Capital	Critical Success Factors
3M	Diversified Manufacturing	• Research & Patents • Global Operations, Distribution Network & Relationships • Brands & Trademark Recognition • Technological & engineering capabilities	• Create market acceptance of new product offerings • Ensure continuity of new product innovation • Supply chain management • Product portfolio management • Information integration and security
Walgreens	Drugstore Chain	• Brands, Trademarks, Patents, Copyrights • Retail drugstore operations expertise • Healthcare service & delivery	• Understand consumers and manage merchandise strategy • Develop private brand products and services • Manage expansion through 3rd parties (i.e. Alliance Boots, AmerisourceBergen)
UPS	Package Delivery	• Global brand & integrated network • Operational efficiency • Transcontinental trade expertise • Segment expertise (i.e. healthcare, high-tech, automotive, etc.) • Proprietary technology	• Deploy technology enabled operations • Understand industry specific needs and design unique logistics solutions • Understand emerging markets and service opportunities • Build and maintain long-term customer relationships

Figure 5.3 Intellectual Capital and Critical Success Factors—Company Examples

Data Source: Respective company annual reports and investor presentations

© 2014 Human Capital Formation, LLC

3M

3M products range from Post-It notes to components for LCD televisions and transdermal drug delivery systems. They cross a multitude of industries and incorporate a great deal of intellectual capital. We calculate their ICI to be 84% of total enterprise value (refer to Figure 3.3, Chapter 3). What makes up all of that intellectual capital? Their IC portfolio is as broad as their industry reach. Driven by $1.7 billion in annual R&D, the company produces a continuous flow of new inventions and patents around the world. Big brands and trademarks such as Scotch, Thinsulate, Post-it, and ACE (bandages) garner consumer loyalty and premium pricing. Some of the major categories that make up 3M intellectual capital, as gleaned from the 10-K and investor presentations, are shown in Figure 5.3.

The first question in Stage 2 of designing a value-driven talent strategy for 3M is, "What do they have to do well to sustain and grow IC?" What are their critical success factors?

Singling out the intellectual capital component, Brands & Trademark Recognition, we could surmise from reviewing public information that a critical success factor for 3M is "Enabling Market Acceptance of New Product Offerings." This would certainly have a positive impact on the value of brands and the 3M trademark. If we were able to look under the hood at 3M, we would likely find a work process called "Channel and Customer Account Management" (or something similar). This would be one of the work processes that contribute to delivering the aforementioned CSF.

If we were to look specifically at 3M's Industrial Business Segment, we may find the position of Senior Product Support Engineer in a part of the organization responsible for channel and customer account management. We may also determine that a Senior Product Support Engineer with aircraft and specialty vehicle expertise is deemed to be critical with respect to enabling customer acceptance of new product offerings in this business segment.

Using this example of Brands & Trademark Recognition for 3M, the resulting workflow for the first stages of building a value-driven talent strategy is illustrated in Figure 5.4. While not having a publicly available value for this IC component, we know from what the company describes that it is significant in the overall $55 billion value of IC. The same method of analysis would be used to identify and connect all of the IC components with CSFs, work processes, and organizations. The critical roles ascertained through this effort carry forward into Stage 3, the determination of talent plans.

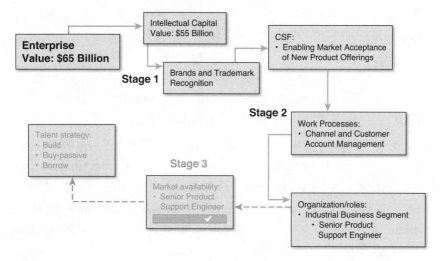

Figure 5.4 3M VTS Example

© 2014 Human Capital Formation, LLC

Walgreen Co.

Next we're moving on to Walgreens at the corner of "Happy and Healthy." A leader in the drugstore industry, Walgreens operates more than 8,000 stores in the United States, many of which are equipped with healthcare clinics and expanding pharmacy operations. Walgreens has expanded its global reach and supply chain capabilities through joint venture relationships with Alliance Boots and AmerisourceBergen.

Commanding an enterprise value of $48 billion, investors recognize Walgreens as a leader by valuing its intellectual capital at $30 billion, or 61% of total enterprise value. This percentage is equivalent to that awarded Walmart and is at the high end of the retail industry. In reviewing Walgreens' 10-K and investor presentations, it is clear that

"Healthcare Service & Delivery" is a large and growing component of their intellectual capital (refer to Figure 5.3).

Digging into the details further, we see that developing and deploying branded products and services such as "Healthcare Clinics and Take Care Employer Solutions" throughout communities in which Walgreens operates is critical to their success in growing the value of "Healthcare Service & Delivery"; let's therefore dub this CSF "Developing Private Brand Products and Services."

I'm speculating, but if we were able to see inside Walgreens, they may have a work process with a name similar to "Product & Services Innovation and Development." This process might guide the development of products and services across the whole organization, or it might be unique to the healthcare business itself, depending on the business strategy and leadership preference.

Taking an additional bit of creative license, let's assume an organization unit exists at Walgreens called "Health and Wellness Solutions," and it contributes, perhaps, along with other organization units to delivering on the CSF of "Developing Private Brand Products and Services." In this organization is the role of "Vice President—Health Innovation." This Vice President has direct responsibility for developing home infusion and respiratory services that are expected to grow significantly and profitably over the next 5–10 years. This is a critical role at Walgreens and will directly contribute to growing the value attributed to the "Healthcare Service & Delivery" component of intellectual capital.

As with the other illustrations, this workflow (shown in Figure 5.5) represents a small slice of the total work. There are undoubtedly many other intellectual capital components, CSFs, work processes, etc. to consider. Also, this is truly just an illustration of the concept drawn from information gathered and surmised about the company.

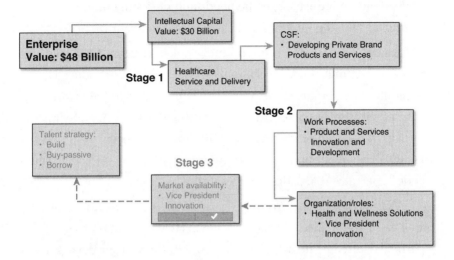

Figure 5.5 Walgreen VTS Example

© 2014 Human Capital Formation, LLC

UPS

As a final example from another industry, UPS surprises some by the depth and breadth of their intellectual capital value. With an enterprise value of $75 billion and 91% ($68 billion) of it made up of IC, UPS truly is a technology company that happens to deliver packages. Some of the aspects driving these amazing values were described in the analysis of UPS in Chapter 3.

Perhaps unbeknownst to the typical UPS customer, the company derives significant value from its "Deep Segment Expertise," which we have named a component of its intellectual capital (refer to Figure 5.3). Its segment expertise spans healthcare, high-tech, and automotive industries, among others, and enables the company to provide customized supply chain solutions that are difficult for competitors to match.

After reviewing UPS public information, we know that to grow the value of "Deep Segment Expertise," UPS must be experts at understanding industry-specific needs and designing unique logistics solutions. This is no doubt a critical success factor for them.

A work process that is important to delivering that CSF might be called something similar to "Supply Chain Solutions Product Development." One organization unit that contributes to this work process might also be called the "Global Accounts Team—Healthcare Sector." The healthcare sector at UPS operates dozens of dedicated health care distribution centers around the world, offering value-added specialized logistics services to the healthcare industry.

Within the "Global Accounts Team-Healthcare Sector" may very well be a role called "Director Global Healthcare Solutions." This particular director likely plays a key role in the further development of the UPS "Temperature True" solution for the storage and shipping of sensitive healthcare products using specialized containers and testing a wide range of refrigeration capabilities. This role contributes directly to the growth of "Deep Segment Expertise" and is critical to continued value creation (see Figure 5.6).

As you can see from these examples, identifying critical success factors, the work processes that support them and, ultimately, the most essential roles, is a key element of the value-driven talent strategy.

From there, the stage is set to invest more in these critical roles to ensure the best talent is acquired and retained so that market capitalization will accelerate. Identifying those roles through the work that's responsible for producing intellectual capital ensures the right investments are made efficiently.

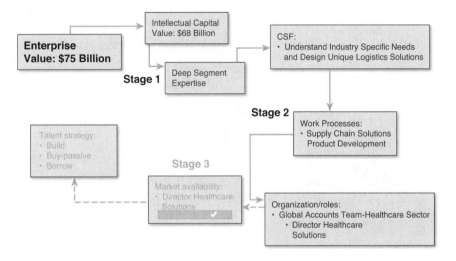

Value-Driven Talent Strategy - Critical Role Workflow
UPS Illustration
Intellectual Capital Component: Deep Segment Expertise

Figure 5.6 UPS VTS Example
© 2014 Human Capital Formation, LLC

Linda: The value-driven talent strategy seems completely counter to how HR functions operate today—generally with a common, enterprise-wide approach to processes like hiring, compensation, performance management, engagement, etc. Doesn't this approach represent too radical a change?

Tom: Unfortunately, for most HR organizations the light at the end of the tunnel is a train. Despite management embracing talent as "the most important asset," budgets for HR are constantly trimmed year after year. These seemingly incongruous facts are not going to change. Without radical adjustment, there is no good ending to the story.

When they say "people are our most important asset," what management really means to say is "we have to grow our value by driving revenue growth and controlling costs, and we need the right talent to do that." But again and again, HR struggles to deliver on that in a way that can be described objectively, with data.

Scarcity of resources is an economic principle that drives allocation to the most valuable use. Spreading HR resources indiscriminately across organizations violates this principle, and the rationale behind doing so is akin to speaking an entirely different language than business leaders. That is the source of the misunderstanding.

The value-driven talent strategy delivers on what management really wants—the right talent—and operates within the principle of scarce resources. It places investment priority where the return is going to be greatest, to the benefit of the entire organization.

More must be invested in critical roles than in other roles; more effective recruiting, more aggressive approaches to compensation and development, and more targeted engagement efforts. Investment in other roles has to be sufficient, but something has to give because the current model isn't driving sustainable, measurable results. If done correctly, the result becomes self-fulfilling, revenue is driven, and the resource pool, although scarce, is expanded.

There is no reason for radical implementation, which never works. An organization should take the model and build a stepped approach where they establish a foundation and build on it toward what ultimately will be an iterative, yet radical, change. The key, however, is beginning with the right skill sets involved—otherwise, the effort is just a set up for disappointing results.

6

The New Talent Strategy Game Plan

- *How can your talent strategy increase business value?*
- *What is the right talent tactic: build, buy, or borrow?*
- *How does talent availability impact planning for critical roles?*
- *What is the right "capital structure" for human capital?*

The value-driven talent strategy (see Figure 6.1) recognizes that a subset of roles is more crucial than all others to producing and sustaining a company's intellectual capital. Because IC is often the largest part of enterprise value, having the right talent in those *critical roles* is a business imperative.

The implication of a value-driven talent strategy is that critical roles require a greater investment than most other roles. Contrary to what has historically been practiced in most companies, higher investment implies that the way talent for critical roles is recruited, developed, measured, rewarded, and retained should be unique to those roles.

In the value-driven talent strategy approach, talent investments are connected directly to market value.

VALUE-DRIVEN TALENT STRATEGY

Company Market Value	Intellectual Capital Value	→	Critical Success Factors (CSF)	Work Processes	→	Critical Talent and Availability Analysis	Talent Strategy Matrix

STAGE 1	STAGE 2	STAGE 3
Connecting talent strategy with value creation begins by understanding the relative importance and composition of intellectual capital within a company's valuation. Intellectual capital value can be calculated using the ICI algorithm (Chapter 2). Components can be identified by evaluating the make up of IC (Chapter 4).	Critical success factors, the things that must be done well, are prioritized by their importance to creating, sustaining, and growing intellectual capital. Priorities vary, especially by industry. Via the work processes associated with high priority CSFs, organization and roles are mapped and categorized.	Roles categorized as critical based on their importance to priority CSFs are set apart. All roles, critical and non-critical, are evaluated for their market availability. Roles are plotted on a four box matrix with axes for Criticality and Market Availability to enable systematic consideration of talent options and actions.

Figure 6.1 Framework: Value-Driven Talent Strategy

© 2014 Human Capital Formation, LLC

What proportion of roles should be considered "critical" in any given organization? The number of critical roles varies with the size and nature of a company's intellectual capital and the way in which it is produced. An industry whose ICI is typically 90% of enterprise value will likely have proportionately more critical roles than those with IC at 50% of enterprise value. The absolute number of critical roles in an organization depends on the scale of the company. However, the number or proportion of critical roles is ultimately less important than the method by which they are identified and leveraged.

In Stage 3 of the value-driven talent strategy approach, critical roles are the focal point for making choices that determine how talent will be supplied. One of the most important considerations is whether to *build, buy,* or *borrow* needed talent.

Let's define these terms:

- **Build**—Developing and retaining talent already employed by the company
- **Buy**—Hiring talent from outside the company
- **Borrow**—Engaging external talent on a temporary basis

When considering each of these options, it's important to weigh the organization's administrative and programmatic capabilities first to assess their likelihood for success. After all, each has distinct requirements to be effectively executed.

For example, for *build* to be a viable primary choice for an organization, the expertise and infrastructure to develop talent must already exist. If this is not the case, then it must first be established, and that has to be factored into the timeline and budget equation. Building talent under any circumstances requires time, discipline, and investment. The result can be highly effective, but it might not be a practical solution for immediate needs or for organizations that don't have a track record of building critical talent from within.

In reality, these choices interact with one another at different points in time. As an example, to build talent, it's necessary to have hired that talent in the first place. You may decide to buy talent that was previously borrowed. A talent strategy allows an organization to plan for and operationalize these choices to satisfy talent needs as they arise. Without such a plan, the build, buy, and borrow options become simply reactionary tactics.

An analysis of the business plan for growth and the talent implications created by that plan can indicate the best build, buy, or borrow approach. A decision tree is useful in thinking through which choice would be most appropriate for a given situation (see Figure 6.2).

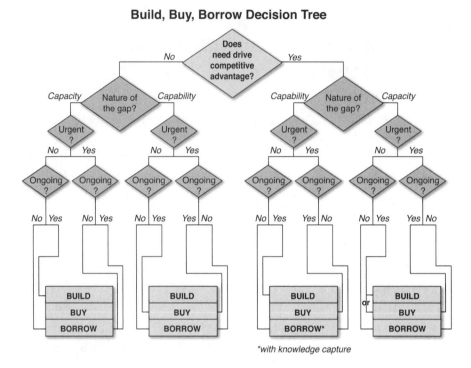

Figure 6.2 Build, Buy, or Borrow Decision Tree
© 2014 Human Capital Formation, LLC

Let's consider each of these choices in context.

Build

Building talent pipelines from within an organization is a strategy to consider particularly if the talent needs are ongoing and critical. It makes the most sense for companies to invest in these roles and ensure incumbents are dedicated, regular employees.

As previously noted, this is an approach best suited for companies with a history of developing talent from within and pools of talent that lend themselves to upward mobility.

Consider the role of Merchant at The Home Depot. Merchants determine the types and quantities of products carried within The Home Depot's retail and online stores. As a relatively small team within the organization, they are responsible for billions of dollars of merchandise and ultimately determine the success of product availability and sales. They must demonstrate a blend of financial and strategic expertise, a deep understanding of the marketplace, and the ability to negotiate and influence vendors and other critical stakeholders. In that department, external hires are brought in as Associate Merchants and, over time, are trained and developed into the Merchant role. From there, top performers are selected to be Department Merchandising Managers and, ultimately, Merchandising Vice Presidents.

In such a structure, the build tactic makes the most sense for the organization. Those who are hired in as Associate Merchants, with the proper training, coaching, and supervision, learn the business and are best suited to excel in higher level roles over time.

Buy

When the need is urgent and ongoing, the most appropriate strategy is typically to acquire talent from the outside. If we stick to our Home Depot example, we can consider the roles of Assistant Store Managers. Let's assume the average Home Depot store employs four Assistant Store Managers. If there were ten stores in a market, then there would be a need for 40 Assistant Store Managers at any one time in that market. If there weren't enough "ready-now" Shift Managers (the role below that of Assistant Store Manager), to fill any open ASM roles, then the company must hire from the outside to fill those roles. Potential candidates might come from Lowe's or other big box retailers such as Best Buy or Target. There is always going to be a need for Assistant Store Managers, and there is always going to be a lot of movement in such an organization due to attrition, promotion, and churn. Therefore, the buy strategy (probably in combination with the build strategy), is a good approach in this example.

Borrow

There are two primary instances when borrowing talent may be the best option for critical roles. These are

- When there is a need to temporarily boost *capacity*
- When a *capability* is required that exceeds or is different from that which is needed on an ongoing basis

With that said, the market for borrowing talent has become more robust and is more often able to supply a wide variety of roles. In some areas, critical skills may be more available via contingent (or borrow) relationships instead of full-time, regular employment. Consider individuals with specialized IT skills that will choose free agent contracts over traditional employment arrangements. In such cases, companies need to adapt their talent tactics to the available labor supply.

The nontraditional talent evolution will continue and expand in future years as the borrow alternative becomes more attractive for both individuals and employers. Consider these trends:

- Forty-four percent of working Americans described themselves as "free agent" workers in a 2011 survey, up from 26% in 2008.[1]
- The professional contingent talent market exceeds $100 billion globally.[2]
- "Free agents" cite work-life balance, schedule flexibility, and work variety as reasons along with ability to earn same or better compensation.
- Fifty-eight percent of U.S. companies expect to use more temporary arrangements at all levels in the years ahead, according to 2011 McKinsey research.[3]

Linda: It seems like "borrow" is always going to be a last resort. Do you really see it as a strategy—or just a tactic?

Tom: Borrowing for professional roles has historically been simply a tactic in most companies. For a variety of reasons, that is changing, and this change benefits both corporations and individual workers.

Corporations have the dilemma of requiring agility while attempting to keep costs low. It is not affordable for most to keep extra headcount onboard to react quickly when business opportunities crop up. Having access to the right quality of temporary talent at a moment's notice is an attractive option.

On the individuals' side, a significant percentage of highly qualified professionals prefer to work on an assignment rather than on a "permanent" basis. It is a lifestyle choice that has developed into a high growth market.

Although most professional contingent workers are still on site, the virtual market is also growing rapidly. Take Elance-oDesk for example. This recently combined duo has more than 9 million high-end professionals in its global online network and 3 million registered client users. The talent in this network, for the most part, works virtually and has skills concentrated in the creative and systems areas. Many Fortune 500 companies tap into this resource. Elance-oDesk has collectively raised over $170 million in venture capital funding.

The global professional contingent workforce exceeds $100 billion in size and is growing. Contingent workers cost less than permanent professionals when all costs are considered and they add flexibility to the organization structure. From a risk/reward standpoint, it is almost irresponsible not to have contingent talent in your workforce plan. Moving forward, borrow should only be considered "just a tactic" for those who are tactical!

Talent Supply and Demand

As we saw in the borrow option, market availability is an important factor impacting build, buy, and borrow choices for all talent categories.

Human capital strategy is ultimately determined through understanding critical needs and the availability of talent to satisfy them. Availability of talent for critical roles varies among the build, buy, and borrow choices for any given talent type. An analysis of each source must be conducted in advance of making final decisions on talent strategy to determine which are truly viable.

To complicate matters, the talent supply might not be in obvious places. For example, knowledge workers do not always have to be physically present to be deployed. Working remotely for knowledge workers is a proven concept, although not universally accepted. In some cases, there are valid reasons why knowledge workers must be physically located in a particular place. But for a growing number of knowledge-based roles, availability is more a matter of time than of physical access.

As a business reality, dollars available to invest in supplying talent to the organization are limited. Practically speaking, talent plans have to prioritize needs based on business value and then differentiate investment according to those needs. Given this reality, roles must first be categorized by their criticality and availability. Next, the appropriate tools and methods to deploy against each category must be determined. The matrix shown in Figure 6.3 is a simple yet effective aid for doing this.

Talent Strategy Matrix

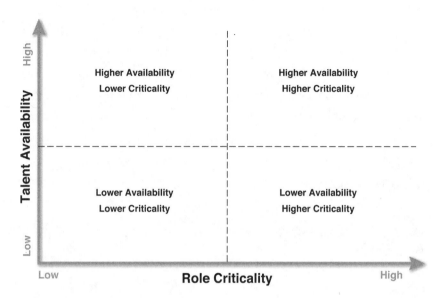

Figure 6.3 Talent Strategy Matrix

© 2014 Human Capital Formation, LLC

We demonstrate the utility of this matrix by referring back to our example of a Senior Product Support Engineer at 3M, which we already determined to be a critical role in Chapter 5, "Identifying Critical Roles Through Work Processes." Considering this critical role and a sample of other hypothetical roles at 3M, we can bring the usefulness of the talent strategy matrix to life. In addition to the Senior Product Support Engineer, we'll assume the roles of Director of International Taxation and Senior Systems Support Manager, both of which have not been designated as critical to 3M but are important. Last, a second critical role, Market Development Manager, will also be added to the mix.

Surveying the market, we determine that the Senior Product Support Engineer (who must have expertise in the aircraft and specialty vehicle areas) is a skillset that is not abundantly available and is in relatively high demand. The Director of International Taxation, while not a "critical" role, is a niche one for which very few qualified candidates exist in the marketplace. The Senior Systems Support Manager is an important role but is a fairly common practice area in most organizations. Last, the Market Development Manager is a critical role (responsible for growing targeted market segments) for which talent is widely available in the marketplace.

We use the talent strategy matrix to work through the implications of what we know about each role (see Figure 6.4), moving counterclockwise starting with the Senior Systems Support Manager.

Senior Systems Support Manager

In our example, this role is not designated as critical at 3M, and our research shows that market availability for this skill set is high. Because of these factors and assuming good performance, we would want to retain and reward the incumbent in this role, but our business risk if we lose them is low. As a result, our talent plans for acquiring or replacing talent in this role is focused externally. Although an appropriate internal replacement would be fine, the circumstances do not demand significant investment in building an internal pipeline for this role. In the event that we have to replace or hire additional capacity in this role, we would use efficient methods of accessing the readily available candidates in the marketplace. Our approach would minimize the search investment by primarily targeting candidates that are actively searching for an opportunity through general advertising and job postings. Employee referral programs can also tap into more passive (not actively looking) candidates.

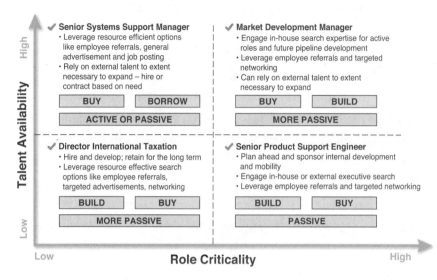

Figure 6.4 Talent Strategy Matrix – 3M
© 2014 Human Capital Formation, LLC

This role also lends itself to considering the borrow option, particularly if the primary need is to increase capacity—and the need is urgent. Part of the talent plan for this and similar roles would be to have relationships in place with individuals or vendors to ensure a reliable supply of contract talent.

Bottom line: There are a variety of low cost options for finding talent in the event that the Senior Systems Support Manager position becomes open.

Director of International Taxation

The availability of talent for this niche role is very limited. Although the role may not be critical to producing the intellectual capital that drives 3M market value, it is an important and indispensable role. Because of this, a practical approach for this role would be to focus on hiring talent into earlier stage positions and developing them for eventual succession. This approach would, of course, rely on the organization's ability to provide an effective development experience and to retain talent throughout the development period.

In the event that an external hire were required to replace or backfill talent in this role, it would be necessary to target passive candidates already employed in similar roles at other companies. Proactively identifying candidates would likely be necessary due to the dearth of talent in the marketplace. Effective means of doing this might include seeking employee referrals, targeting advertising in relevant professional media, and tapping into networks (personal or professional) that include taxation professionals. It may even be necessary to use a specialized search firm to find this external talent.

Bottom line: There are relatively few options for finding suitable talent should this role become open, and each requires time and investment.

Senior Product Support Engineer

This is our most challenging role. The role is critical to creating value and because further specialized knowledge is needed, candidates in the marketplace are few and far between. Suffice it to say, we are prepared to make our biggest investment in this type of role.

If we are able to forecast and strategically plan for these roles, the primary focus (although not exclusively) should be on developing talent internally. These roles produce a level of value that merits investing in exceptional programs to develop and retain them. I was told by the Engineering leader at a prominent corporation that it takes approximately eight years to develop engineering talent to that firm's specifications. A program to achieve a result like that must be well resourced and flawlessly executed. Losing talent after a few years in such a scenario would be devastating.

When the need arises to hire external talent into a critical role for which availability of candidates is limited (inevitable at some point!), passive candidates must be targeted. Research shows that normally more than 50% of the market is passive, and that number no doubt increases significantly when candidates are in short supply. It is reasonable to assume that passive candidates are currently employed and fully engaged; they will have to be identified, attracted, and sold on a new and better opportunity. This requires direct search capability either in-house or through a third-party search firm.

Bottom line: With even fewer options for finding suitable talent for this role, the organization must invest time and money into longer term plays that involve either development (and retention) from within or external candidate research and pipelining.

Market Development Manager

Research shows that although this role is critical to producing value at 3M, there is a good supply of talent with this skill set in the market. The first priority should be establishing the ability to tap the external market for this talent. In-house sourcing capability is ideal in this situation because of the opportunity to continuously pipeline available external talent as a supply strategy. Because the role is critical, available, and not a temporary need, borrowing is not a desirable alternative. Though there is always value in building talent for critical roles, excessive investment in building pipelines in this scenario is not crucial given talent for this role is widely available.

Bottom line: There are multiple options to find suitable talent for this role; however, because the role is critical, passive candidates should be sought if searching externally to maximize the pool size and consequent quality of hire.

In-House Search Expertise

The trend of companies to build their own in-house search functions, rather than relying on outside search firms, is growing. There is an obvious opportunity for lowering costs, but even more importantly, if done well, in-house search capability increases the quality of hire over that of external search firms. The reasons in-house search can deliver better quality are simple:

- The company can employ the same level of search talent (without a markup for profit margin).

- In-house search teams are more knowledgeable about the culture and literally have to live with the results of their hiring recommendations.

- They are focused on one "client" and one industry—that of their employer—instead of many.

- There are no "off limits" with other client companies.

- They are not pressured to fill requisitions for billing purposes.

Companies dedicated to the process of bringing search in-house recognize the strategic need for building this competency within their business. They understand the value of owning and growing the expertise for finding critical talent. In addition, the data that is generated through such work efforts (e.g., market research, competitive analysis, databases of potential candidates) in and of itself is valuable intellectual capital.

For these reasons, it makes sense to invest in in-house search capability if the transaction volume, including pipeline requirements, provides sufficient scale. An added advantage of building search capability for critical roles is the trickle down impact to the rest of the recruiting function. The entire Talent Acquisition function tends to become more proficient as a result of this leading edge activity that often involves best-in-class research, sourcing, and selection methods.

Compensation Decisions

Another important aspect of talent strategy that the matrix helps put into perspective is compensation. Because most organizations have not historically analyzed talent needs against the business value they create, they are likely to be overpaying for some roles and underpaying for others. This dilemma has been driving the debate over "A" versus "B" players for decades. Many companies attempt to pay professionals with similar tenure and qualifications about the same regardless of their value to the business. These efforts are aided by salary surveys and market studies conducted by internal comp teams or external HR consulting firms—none of which portend to gauge relative value for particular firms and industries. In the end, however, these attempts at being "fair" distract or even impede the securing of talent for the most value-driving roles in the business.

The approach to both compensation strategy in general and role-specific pay decisions in particular begins to look very different when there is a clear picture of talent availability and its relative value to the business. It is easy to pay more than you have to for certain skill sets, but it is not necessary. It may even be affordable to do so in the short run, but there is no shortage of examples where this catches up with companies sooner or later and forces other bad decisions such as across the board cost cutting (that is, indiscriminately from a business value standpoint). With the knowledge of role criticality and market availability, companies can create a better balance in compensation that affords adequate talent in less critical roles while competing more effectively for top talent in critical roles (see Figure 6.5)

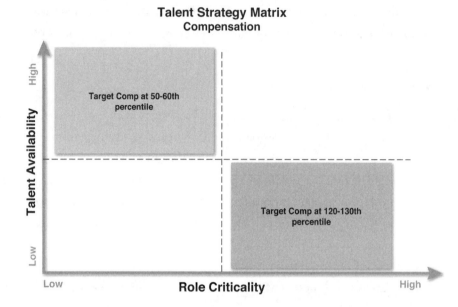

Figure 6.5 Rationalizing Compensation for Criticality
© 2014 Human Capital Formation, LLC

Build, Buy, Borrow and the Capital Structure of Talent

The world economy, the way in which value is created, and how work gets done has changed dramatically. There's been an enormous evolution: from labor to knowledge workers, lifelong to "at will" employment, and from employment itself to contingent services. Yet throughout, the capital structure of talent (or, more accurately, human capital) has remained largely unchanged. At its most basic level, many companies still operate in a *full-time equivalent* (FTE) world—as they have for decades. In this world, annual budget decisions regarding headcount are made based on projected work—hiring requisitions are opened, jobs are posted, and new "permanent" employees are chosen. Discussions or decisions regarding the best approach—build, buy, borrow—typically don't take place because such activity happens in the absence of a talent strategy linked to business value.

In our knowledge economy, this model isn't simply flawed; it impedes the creation of business value. Therefore, an entirely new way of thinking about human capital structure is required for businesses to adapt and thrive.

Before going further, consider how the other capital, financial capital, has structurally evolved and why. Virtually all companies today carry a measurable percentage of debt to shareholder equity in their capital structure. This is often a percentage in the range of 25% or greater depending on multiple factors including type of industry and, certainly, tolerance for risk.

Choosing debt rather than equity is intentional. Although debt bears interest and must be repaid on schedule, somewhat counter intuitively, debt is normally less expensive than equity. Debt acts to lower the total cost of capital for a corporation. When all is said and done, because shareholders expect their shares to appreciate and to pay dividends, the cost of equity capital typically exceeds 10%. The cost of debt for a healthy company is often a fraction of that amount.

There is more flexibility with debt than there is with equity. Debt can be more easily increased or decreased in response to changing business requirements or economic conditions than equity (which requires time-consuming regulatory and registration procedures). When the opportunity to acquire business assets or take advantage of an unfolding market opportunity suddenly arises, debt capital can be quickly accessed and deployed. Likewise, in a market downturn with rising interest rates, debt can be reduced as necessary.

It is also advantageous that adding debt does not dilute voting power in financial capital structure. The relative voice that existing shareholders have in the business remains unchanged.

Although debt offers many benefits to capital structure, its primary role is to supplement shareholder equity, not replace it. Although the long-term cost of capital for equity is higher than for debt, in the short run equity holders provide more stability because their interests rest as much with growing the value of the business as they do with receiving payout in the form of dividends. In fact, loading up a business with too much debt can result in a company's credit rating and securities being reduced to "junk" status.

Herein lies the resemblance between the choices for financial capital and those for human capital. The table in Figure 6.6 provides specific comparisons.

Overall, borrowing talent is less expensive than buying it which shows similarities when comparing those choices with aspects of financial capital structure in Figure 6.6. Borrowing talent or capital also offers more flexibility and control to the company. But despite these benefits when it comes to financial capital structure, companies are careful to not lever it too much with debt. Financially, the cash flow imperative of debt is a main concern. And fundamentally, the motivation of equity holders is more aligned with the interests of the business; this holds true in the case of employment as well. Given all this, what is a rational way for companies to think about the right mix of employee and contingent talent to optimize the efficiency and effectiveness of its human capital structure?

Rather than accepting the use of contingent talent as simply a default solution to urgent capacity needs, broader consideration must be given to this topic. The objective should be to understand what roles and circumstances merit consideration for being supplied with contingent talent. One survey by the Aberdeen Group reported that 26% of the average organization's workforce is already effectively contingent.[4] I suspect that evaluating any given organization from top to bottom may yield surprising results. In the absence of a contingent talent strategy there are likely to be roles staffed with contingent talent that should not be and vice versa.

A New Capital Structure for Human Capital? *Contrasting **Equity and Debt** with **Employee and Contingent** talent*		
Characteristic	**Equity and Debt**	**Employee and Contingent**
Cost	Over time, equity has a higher cost than debt; shareholders expect both risk-adjusted share appreciation and dividend growth.	Employment is higher cost than contingency; the combination of salary, benefits, bonus, stock and development, total more in the long run.
	Debt has a cash cost of interest and principle that must be paid timely to avoid default. Although the economic cost is lower than equity, near term cash cost is inflexible.	Contingent services can have a higher immediate cash cost than employment, although in the long run, total cost is less. This cash cost is relatively fixed compared to variable employment compensation.
Control	Equity holders having voting rights based on the number of shares held.	Employees have a broad set of unstated "voting rights" evidenced by engagement surveys and various forums for considering their thoughts and suggestions.
	Debt holders do not have voting rights.	Contingent workers do not normally participate in employee engagement forums (and don't expect to).
Flexibility	Equity takes time to raise due to regulatory requirements and investor communication needs ---- this process can easily take 6-12 months.	The hiring process for professional roles will typically require 60-120 days to start a new employee.
	Regulatory requirements for debt are lower and less time consuming than for equity. Lines of credit can be set up in advance of need.	Contingent service workers can be contracted almost immediately. Suppliers can be set up ahead of time.
Convertibility	Not applicable for equity.	Not applicable for employee.
	Debt can be structured with a convert option to equity. This makes the investment more attractive to holders.	Contingent workers can convert to employment at a later stage. This is a viable external sourcing strategy.
Engagement	Equity holders are the key targets of Investor Relations efforts. IR engages and retains holders by keeping them motivated about investment potential.	Effectively retaining talent requires concerted and continuous dialogue regarding benefits of employment (see the Human Capitalist Investor in Chapter 8).
	IR spends minimal time with debt holders. Debt holders are focused on receiving interest and principal payment.	Contingent workers require reliable payment for services but minimal engagement efforts.
Term	While shares circulate freely in the market, large equity holders often choose to hold quality stocks for the long term. Companies invest in retaining these shareholders.	Employees are deemed to be "permanent" (although less so than in the past). Companies strive to retain critical talent.
	While it may stretch over a period of years, debt capital is normally fixed term.	Contingent workers are normally contracted for a fixed period of time or until defined work is delivered.
Transaction Costs	The transaction cost of raising equity is high, including registering securities, legal and banker fees, and stock exchange fees.	The cost of hiring can be steep including search fees, hiring bonuses, relocation costs and make-whole payments.
	The transaction cost of debt is less than equity due to lower regulatory and exchange costs.	The transaction cost of engaging contingent services is normally limited to agency fees if applicable.
Investor Risk	The inherent risk of owning equity is higher than debt. Return on equity depends on long-term success. Also, equity holders are behind debt holders in claims on the corporation in a bankruptcy.	The risk to employment is higher than the risk to contingent work per se. Employees' outcomes are linked directly to the companies'.
	Debt holders' claims take precedent in bankruptcy. Because of this, the risk associated with debt is lower (and overall returns required of equity are higher).	Contingent workers are compensated by an agreed amount of cash. They don't normally bear the same risk as employees with respect to variances in the value of performance based compensation and stock.

Figure 6.6 Contrasting Financial with Human Capital Structure

As previously discussed, it's relatively easy to categorize roles according to their criticality and market availability. This is a good starting point for thoroughly considering the best use of contingent talent.

In our Build, Buy, Borrow Decision Tree (shown in Figure 6.2), if the answer to the question, "Is the talent need ongoing?" is no, then borrowing talent is the logical approach. Data indicates that more and more roles are not in fact as "ongoing" as they used to be, but often almost cyclical, yet still thought of and staffed as "permanent." Circumstances that lend themselves well to the borrow option include the following:

- Noncritical roles—additional capacity
- Noncritical roles—individual contributors
- Critical roles—some additional capacity needs
- Project management roles
- Leading edge niche skill sets

Circumstances that do not lend themselves well to the borrow option:

- Core critical roles
- Low availability noncritical roles
- Leadership roles

Linda: Many HR functions don't handle the "borrow" (contingent talent) decisions; it's done by Procurement. Isn't there value in Procurement overseeing these big expenditures?

Tom: It is true that HR functions do not typically have the expertise to negotiate significant third-party supply contracts. When an agency is selected to secure contingent talent, I would expect Procurement to be involved. The same holds true for negotiating significant contracts with executive search firms, by the way.

But in both cases, HR must define the terms of what is being bought. Contingent talent is clearly a component of the workforce, and determinations regarding the profile request, selection requirements, service level agreements, etc. is the expertise of HR, not Procurement. Once those terms are agreed upon, Procurement is well-suited to negotiate the price and other economic terms as long as they do not negatively impact delivery. Therefore, in such an engagement, HR and Procurement should work closely together.

As an aside, it is difficult to routinely hire contingent labor in the U.S. without using an intermediary agency because of existing employment law risk. Co-employment risk, basically a non-employee being deemed an employee and due retroactive benefits along with other penalties, is a serious barrier to direct contingent talent agreements for companies.

With the growth rate in contingent talent usage, I would expect to see a regulatory environment, at some point in the future, that enables companies to directly recruit and contract contingent talent just as they do with regular employees today. That would lower the landed cost of contingent talent and no doubt enable even greater growth of this talent segment. Of course for HR, it will mean acquiring and learning how to execute yet another new capability.

The Importance of Talent Planning

Given employment and talent trends, there is untapped value in talent planning. For example, as already noted, it would be a valuable exercise for companies to assess how value is created, which functions and roles create the most value, the availability of talent versus criticality of specific roles, and the viability for using contingent talent rather than employee talent to fill certain roles.

Just one element along this talent planning continuum—the contingent labor question—can allow an organization to efficiently expand and contract with business needs in the same way that financial capital can.

It is worthwhile to intentionally plan a strategic mix between employee talent and contingent talent. By doing so, companies take a step in the right direction to optimize organization cost, flexibility, and effectiveness for the long term.

Designing the mix of employee and contingent talent will yield the following:

- Better aligned interests of talent with interests of the company
- Maximized access to the talent market in all its forms for the right roles
- Improved ability to expand and contract with the market and economic trends

On this last point alone, given the billions of dollars in "one-time" downsizing costs incurred every year, there is surely an opportunity to intentionally structure for ups and downs in business cycles that will benefit both financial and human capital investors—a new, cost-efficient capital structure for human capital.

Endnotes

1. Kelly Services 2011 Free Agent Survey.
2. Calculated from Adecco Holdings 2012 Annual Report.
3. "The Rise of the Supertemp," *Harvard Business Review*, Miller and Miller, 2012.
4. Aberdeen Group, "Contingent Workforce Management: The Next-Generation Guidebook to Managing the Modern Contingent Workforce Umbrella," May 2012.

7

The Only Metric that Matters

- *Overview of metrics*
- *Defining quality*
- *Measuring quality*
- *Raising the quality metric*

There are dozens of measurements that are important to the overall effort of managing talent. After all, talent management is a complex process that spans the entire employment life cycle and includes planning, acquiring, developing and retaining talent. As with any process, there are expectations for effectiveness and efficiency and a need to measure both to properly evaluate results and to drive continuous improvement. Looking across the talent management spectrum at activities such as recruitment, development and compensation, it is obvious there are many subprocesses intended to work together to achieve the goals of talent management. At different stages in each of these subprocesses, outputs are produced that should be measured to provide the means for managing overall process effectiveness.

To illustrate this concept, imagine driving a manual shift transmission automobile down a deserted highway. On this highway, the speed limit is marked 70 mph, and signs also note that the minimum speed is 40 mph. If your priority were to drive this stretch of road in an *effective* way, you would simply stay within this speed range. If you also wanted to be *efficient*, you would focus on optimizing your fuel usage too.

But in reality, as you drive your car, there are many subprocesses that have an impact on your ability to maintain speed within the desired range while optimizing fuel usage. Trying to maintain this speed in second gear would send your rpms through the roof and eventually overheat your engine, so a tachometer helps you monitor this. Engine temperature can be impacted by other issues (such as coolant levels), and overheating can stop you in your tracks, so there is a temperature gauge. Oil supply to the engine is essential, and therefore you can keep an eye on your oil level measurement as well. Each of these and other subprocesses are essential to being able to achieve the effectiveness and efficiency goals that you have set. In addition, in your vehicle, each of these subprocesses has a target built into their measurement, creating a metric.

Like this example of driving an automobile, measuring talent management subprocesses—such as the time it takes to fill a vacant role or the range of performance review scores—can tell an important story about how efficient and effective we are at managing talent. Without a doubt, there are dozens of subprocess measurements that are important to managing the overall talent process. But the strategic objectives of the entire, connected talent process dictate which are the most essential metrics to achieve.

So, in a world driven by knowledge, what are the strategic objectives of the talent process, and how do we differentiate between the "oil gauge" and "speedometer" as measurement tools to successfully guide us? Like any complex process, there are many data points that matter; the rest of this chapter will deal with identifying and measuring the ones that matter the most.

Linda: All I know is, when I'm driving, I don't want to run out of gas. If I'm a CEO, is there an analogy for talent management? What's the most important HR metric that I need to be monitoring constantly?

Tom: The CEO doesn't want to run out of gas either! The CEO has a clear vision of where the enterprise is headed and what it will take to get there. The CEO's task is to convey this vision to the management team and organization at large so they can do the things necessary to realize that vision. When it comes to talent, the CEO must rely—to some extent—on managers and HR to anticipate needs accurately and achieve the vision through talent. Think of the analogies to the talent dilemma a CEO faces in fueling their organization: Do we drive development from within? Or hire from outside? (Diesel or regular?) Do we invest in high potential programs? Or improved onboarding? (High test or ethanol?) Is our talent pool deep enough? (How many gallons to fill the tank?) CEOs may look to HR for direction, but they also know that in this world of dependence on human capital for growth, delegating all responsibility for talent is risky business.

PWC's 17th annual survey of CEOs (2014) summarizes the CEOs' perspective very well:

Concern?

—63% said availability of skills was a serious concern

What are they going to do about it?

—93% said they recognize the need to change their strategy for attracting and retaining talent.

How are they going to do that?

—Only 34% feel that HR is ready for the task.

So, from the perspective of CEOs, the *most important metric* to monitor is the availability of quality talent—but their *biggest concern* is HR's ability to do something about it.

CEOs will have to demand the creation of measurable, business-based talent strategies in order to close this gap. When given the opportunity, most CEOs are fully engaged in the strategic discussion about critical success factors and the roles that are most important to achieving them. HR needs to bring this thinking to the table and facilitate such discussions.

In the end, it's the quality of talent that matters above all other human capital metrics. As Ray Kroc simply stated, "You're only as good as the people you hire."[1]

Ultimately, the dozens of talent management subprocesses must holistically produce efficiency and effectiveness outcomes that meet (or exceed) an organization's talent requirements. To improve performance, an organization must be able to evaluate the subprocess metrics and results to find improvement opportunities. As with all processes, the subprocesses accumulate to the highest-level categories of effectiveness and efficiency measured as quality, time, and cost. The process challenge lies in optimizing these three measures for the best outcome ("pick any two" is the oft-quoted engineering retort to the idea of optimizing them all). What do quality, time, and cost mean in the context of talent?

Talent quality, the speed with which talent decisions are made, and the costs associated with such efforts are all important factors. But if we think of business activity as a series of investments that deploy both financial and human capital, what types of results should we look for? How do speed, cost, and quality impact these results?

Let's take the hypothetical example of a pharmaceutical company investing in an initiative to develop a new drug that will require FDA approval to go to market (see Figure 7.1). Millions of dollars of financial capital will be necessary for the initial investment required to develop the product. We know that developing a new drug requires a massive amount of research at many levels and stages. The research will inform product development followed by intensive testing and adjustment. Regulatory review, testing, and management are extensive and complex. After years of development, a successful product launch requires accurate planning and further investment in production capacity and know-how.

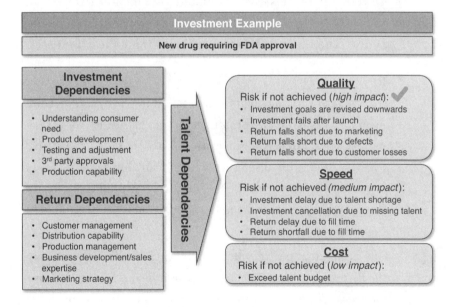

Figure 7.1 The Impact of Talent on Investment Returns
© 2014 Human Capital Formation, LLC

Millions more will be wrapped up in taking the new drug to market to earn a return. Success in the market will require execution capability to ensure the product has distribution through the right channels, uninterrupted supply, and clear and compelling communication to the target audience and stakeholders.

Most of the financial capital required to drive a positive return on this investment bet will be used to fund human capital.

In this context, let's look again at cost, speed, and quality.

- **Cost**

  The cost of ensuring the right talent is available at the right time to execute this investment, while not insubstantial, is small relative to the multiple millions required for a successful product introduction. Therefore, even if the recruiting and selection effort to support this work amounted to $2 million and the team went over budget by 20%, it's pennies compared to the larger picture. Therefore, in this scenario, cost is not the priority.

- **Speed**

  The impact of not having the right talent in place *on time* could be material to the investment and return results. A case in point: Check Point Systems suffered a 20% hit to their stock price in 2006 after disclosing a significant hiring miss, which imperiled expected sales results and forced public disclosure. The company's market value dropped by nearly $200 million in a single day.[2]

  This is an example of when a lack of available talent delays the investment timeline, causing significant financial consequences. An extreme situation could even result in cancelation of the entire investment (and opportunity lost to competition). Slow hiring during implementation and launch could delay the expected return and even permanently decrease it. So, clearly the timing dimension of talent is very important to this investment—and more important than cost considerations.

- **Quality**

  Above all, the impact of talent quality has the greatest potential to determine success or failure of an investment. Significant bets carry significant expectations and requirements. Talent deployed on time, at the right cost, but not fully up to the task will likely have a permanent impact on the investment outcome and require goals to be revised downward. When this occurs, it puts pressure on every subsequent dollar invested, and the negative impact can easily snowball. In the worst-case scenario (which can happen in the best of worlds), the investment will fail before or even after it is launched, burning the entire invested amount. Talent not fully up to the task can have an equally disastrous impact on the execution side of marketing, quality control, customer management and other critical activities, destroying the value of an otherwise solid investment. It is also important to bear in mind that value creation is an ongoing cycle; in addition to a standalone outcome, any one investment delivers knowledge that can be reinvested in other initiatives. The value of this knowledge is proportional to the quality of talent accumulating it.

Talent quality problems are usually not publicized and often not even specifically recognized inside of organizations for reasons ranging from their sensitive personal nature to the absence of measurement standards. However, there are plenty of red flags to look for, including:

- Increased frequency of underperforming new products (for example, recall frequency among automobile manufacturers)
- Negative change in company financial and market performance versus industry competitors over a sustained period (Circuit City vs. Best Buy, J.C. Penney vs. Target, Zenith vs. Sony)

- Failure to evolve business direction in the face of mega-trend industry changes (Polaroid, Kodak, Blockbuster)
- Increased turnover in core talent areas (see reviews and trends on sites such as Glassdoor)

The scale of the impact talent quality has on investment results makes it "the only metric that matters" in an intellectual capital world.

Which leads us to the question: How is talent quality defined?

There are many views about what defines talent quality. An "A" player in *Topgrading*, for example, is judged on criteria that include intelligence, leadership, drive, resourcefulness, and team building, among others.[3] Corporate Executive Board (CEB) defines quality of hire as being "meaningful along two dimensions: the sheer output—that is, the performance itself—and the time during which that performance is measured, for which attraction/retention serves as a proxy."[4]

Alternatively, I believe the quality of talent, specifically for knowledge workers, is the measure of an individual's ability to generate intellectual capital over a sustained period of time. High quality talent presents itself as a blend of specific skills along with the means to drive valuable results within the context of a particular organization. The "particular organization" component is why top talent isn't necessarily transferrable from one organization to another. Talent quality cannot exist in the absence of positive results, to state the obvious.

There are numerous high profile examples of leaders who have performed very well at top name corporations, only to fail dramatically when transplanted to other industries; Bob Nardelli from GE to Home Depot and Ron Johnson from Apple to J.C. Penney are two well-known examples.

Harvard Business School's Boris Groysberg weighs in on the issue of firm specific knowledge in his recent book, *Chasing Stars*: "According to proponents of human-capital theory, mastery of the idiosyncrasies of a particular work setting is a sine qua non of high productivity, but the set of skills that constitutes such mastery has no value outside the firm."[5] Point being, the value of individual competencies, especially those that are more firm-specific, is often contextual.

Linda: This seems to fly in the face of the old hiring adage, "Past performance is the best indicator of future performance." Is the common practice of hiring individuals who've done well at a competitor—or in another industry—a flawed one?

Tom: I think past performance is a good starting point as long as you understand what is required of future performance and are able to assess for that. If someone is coming into a company from outside, in addition to whatever technical expertise is required, they will have to be able to adapt to and thrive in a new culture. If they are coming from another industry, they must be skilled at evaluating and judging new situations in order to productively apply their knowledge and experience in a different environment. How well have they done that in the past? Do they have a track record, or is this unknown territory? I think past performance is a very relevant consideration but, as it relates to future performance in a new company, nothing can be assumed.

Linda: Is this more about how they've done it versus what they've done?

Tom: Yes, first and foremost. The "how" is a more revealing conversation in my experience. "How did you do it? What were the results? What did you learn?" This combination gets at behavioral qualities and an individual's personal formula for success. This provides a pretty good sense of how someone will square up with a particular organization and culture.

In reality, although failures at the CEO level are more publicized, lots of organizations reject new (or recent) hires at all levels. It is a common occurrence to hire on skills and fire on fit.

If you think about heart transplants, the recipient of the first one in 1967 survived for just 18 days. Today the procedure is almost routine and recipients survive more than 15 years on average. Doctors have figured out how to "prescreen" (tissue typing) and "onboard" (immunosuppressants) hearts. There is still a lot of improvement to be made on both those fronts when it comes to transplanting talent from one industry to another.

Knowing Quality When We See It

How can talent quality be observable when one is producing something that is invisible? Understanding the productivity of knowledge workers is the challenge to understanding quality.

Intellectual capital is created when human capital is deployed through work processes in a way that leverages critical success factors. By doing so, an intangible asset (a patent, brand, customer relationship, and so on) is generated or enhanced. But how do we know how productive the talent en masse—or individually—is?

Four data elements measure talent quality on an individual level, which can then be extrapolated on a larger (that is, department or function) scale: performance, potential, promotion, and retention.

The following sections describe recommendations for measuring each.

Performance

No matter how you cut it, how well an individual has performed is an essential data point when measuring talent quality. Performance information reflects current and historic productivity. We know that well-run companies have approaches to performance measurement that range from traditional and formal to avant-garde or crowd-sourced. For the purpose of assessing talent quality, however, any approach is fine as long as it differentiates performance.

Despite having abandoned formal performance reviews, Netflix somehow strictly assesses talent performance if it is true, as quoted in *Harvard Business Review*, that "adequate performance gets a generous severance package."[6] In the same *HBR* article, the author goes on to quote Netflix further: "In many functions—sales, engineering, product development—it's fairly obvious how well people are doing. (As companies develop better analytics to measure performance, this becomes even truer.)" I agree. There are undoubtedly decades of process improvement ahead for defining and measuring performance, particularly for knowledge workers.

Linda: In theory, this makes sense. But in practice, performance measures are rife with imperfect ratings influenced by favoritism, less tenured managers who don't know the performance of their team well, lack of accurate and timely data, and so on. Isn't this a shaky foundation to rest your talent quality measurement on?

Tom: Performance measurement systems are in place in most companies. Although they may not be perfectly designed to measure quality in many cases, they offer a move in the right direction when used consistently. The evolution of the manager's role in performance management is what is more concerning and at the heart of data imperfections, especially with respect to critical talent. The role of manager as simply a "boss" does not require a performance management system. However, the role of manager in applying knowledge to knowledge *does* require such a system. When people served machines and the task was given and obvious, a boss was appropriate. In a knowledge economy—where machines serve people—the worker must determine the task based on clearly stated expectations and outcomes (that is, objectives). This is the role of modern managers—and it requires knowledge and leadership expertise. Managers today must be developed and selected accordingly—based on this new criteria and business reality. Enabling managers (in a scalable, measurable way) is a cornerstone to measuring and growing talent quality and market capitalization.

Linda: What's a company with an imperfect performance review process to do?

Tom: Use the process in place, calibrate talent consistently to the extent possible, and drive continuous process improvements along the way. In the meantime, employees within a company will be assessed according to the same (albeit, perhaps, imperfect) standards. There is still value in such data, particularly where differentiation exists.

Regardless of the structural method of gathering performance data, more importantly, leaders must have the ability to set direction and manage successful outcomes. Performance in many critical roles cannot be directly measured by dollars produced or saved. This is where leaders need the ability to articulate expectations for critical roles and the difference between "adequate," "good," and "great" performance. The ability of leaders to articulate expectations and manage performance is essential in the chain of events that create value. The reality is that a single weak link breaks this chain. And for critical roles, less than a zero-defects chain impacts market value.

Potential

Estimating potential can be more powerful than determining performance. It is a future-oriented view of an individual's longer-term productivity. Organizations that currently utilize potential ratings consider factors including past and current performance, capabilities exhibited (including fit within the organization), and the individual's expressed desires. Sometimes, more elaborate methods are used to evaluate potential, such as simulation-based assessment centers.

In many organizations, evaluation of potential takes place among a certain level of employees—typically wide but not deep. Therefore, a particular company may assess the potential ratings of all Vice Presidents and, based on this data, may determine successors for higher-level roles. This isn't a bad practice, but organizations should also be identifying successors and gathering data about the bench for other mission-critical roles. In addition to going wide, organizations should go deep into targeted areas with critical roles that drive the most value—even if that includes low level yet essential pipeline roles.

Promotion

Whether an individual has been promoted within a certain period of time is a tangible data point indicating productivity. Significant pay adjustments that are not technically promotions may also be tangible data points.

Retention

Retention data—simply knowing who remains with the organization and who has left, regardless of the reasons—is essential to assessing talent quality. Retention data and trends help organizations understand the value of the talent investments and the effectiveness of the process. The implication of retention issues, especially among critical talent, can range from gaps in the hiring process to the engagement strategy, onboarding, or leadership quality.

The use of these four data points allows organizations to apply their best knowledge of historical and future performance, reinforced by tangible recognition, and factoring in sustainability (retention).

In my own experience, I implemented a quality calculation for executive hiring at Coca-Cola that was featured in a CEB case study in 2013.[7] In that effort we tracked the quality elements just mentioned, in addition to other specific goals for our talent pool (see Figure 7.2). All of the data we used was housed in either our SAP or Applicant Tracking systems and was relatively easy to pull together. One of the key uses of the quality indicators at the time was to evaluate how we performed when we directly sourced our own executive talent compared to the use of external search firms. The results of our analysis proved that we sourced measurably higher quality talent using our in-house team.

With respect to measuring talent quality, a key is to allow for the passage of time. If talent quality is ultimately defined as sustained productivity, it requires time to be revealed and observed. In the case of new hires, it takes a significant period of time to settle a person effectively into the organization. Depending on the resources dedicated to achieving a rapid assimilation, a period of at least several quarters is typically required before one can become fully productive. In my experience, 24 months is probably the shortest period of time for which quality data is meaningful. Because of that, I advocate an approach that captures a qualitative snapshot soon after hire via manager feedback as well as structured observations followed by quantitative measurement after the passage of time.

ASSERT A QUALITY (NOT JUST COST) ADVANTAGE

Coca-Cola's Quality-Focused Business Case for In-House Executive Recruiting

Illustrative

> Coca-Cola's executive recruiting function **presents a quality-focused business case to build business leader trust in the team's ability to deliver highest quality talent.**

- Coca-Cola tracks and presents the performance ratings, potential succession ratings, turnover, and diversity of its new executive hires.

- The quality-focused business case corrects business leader misperception that higher-cost executive search firms deliver higher quality talent.

- Hiring managers who understand the quality advantage of the in-house team more effectively work with their executive recruiters.

🌐 **Global Differentiator**

Coca-Cola's executive recruiting team builds credibility with senior line managers around the world using its track record of success in similar markets.

Typical Hiring Leader Attitude Towards In-House Team

We need high-quality talent, so let's go to search.

With this attitude, the hiring manager:

- Accepts higher cost believing its yields higher quality

- Leverages in-house recruiting team for cost savings only

In-House Executive Recruiting Value Proposition: Delivering the Quality You Need

Key Quality of Hire Indicators	Hires sourced by the in-house team	Hires sourced by search firms
Performance	1.2x	x
Potential	2x	x
Turnover	0.6x	x
Diversity	1.2x	x

We charge 15% of the new executive's starting salary to cover headcount and costs.

Coca-Cola measures quality of hire objectively by tracking four key metrics that have direct business implications.

The fee drives commitment from the hiring leader and places the requisite pressure on the in-house team to offer a commercially viable product.

The team often presents its business case to leaders within the organization who are considering their executive search options.

Coca-Cola's Hiring Leader Attitude Towards In-House Team

We need to improve quality, so let's go in-house.

With this attitude, the hiring manager:

- Believes in-house executive recruiting yields higher quality

- Relies on in-house recruiters for search strategy and execution

| SITUATION | OVERVIEW | EXECUTIVE RECRUITER PAIRINGS | SPEED TO EXPERTISE FRAMEWORK | COMBINATION TOOL USE | QUALITY-CENTRIC VALUE PROPOSITION | RESULTS |

Figure 7.2 Measuring Executive Hire Quality at Coca-Cola

© CEB, Quality-Driven Executive Recruiting Function, Arlington VA, 2013, Page 7

I am convinced that these early attempts to measure and manage quality are essential to truly accelerating market value through talent. Organizations should move firmly to institute even more robust and instructive measurement systems. First of all, the quality measurement system must incorporate internal talent as well as external hires. Also, quality measurement should be expressed as an index of sorts— a measure that can standalone as an absolute number and be easily compared to prior periods to track the overall change. The index itself should be a data tool that can be easily dissected into slices and provide insight and aid in identifying process and market opportunities for improvement.

The prototype described on the next few pages meets all the criteria just mentioned. This weighted quality index (WQI) defines levels of quality as combinations of performance, potential, promotion, and retention and is weighted by assigning a productivity factor to each level (see Figure 7.3). A higher productivity factor associated with each higher level of quality yields a weighted calculation of the index. This in turn provides an absolute metric representing quality achieved during a period of time and opens the door for systematic improvement.

The four quality levels in the WQI are named: Superstar, Star, Average, and Below. This model assumes a 4-point scale for rating both performance and potential, a defined set of minimum criteria for reaching each "Quality Level," and the requirement of at least 24 months in the role. The productivity factors assigned to each quality level are based on a CEB case example for differences in productivity between high and low performance of computer programmers.[8] Although this may seem arbitrary when related to other roles, it is nonetheless a data source and a legitimate benchmark.

Defining Quality

Define Super Star, Star, Average, Below Average				
	← Criteria at 24 Months Tenure →			
Quality (Productivity) Level*	**Performance**	**Potential**	**Promotion**	**Retention**
SUPER STAR (12X)	Greatly Exceeds	High	Yes	Yes
STAR (3X)	Exceeds	Promotable	No	Yes
AVERAGE (1X)	Meets	Well Placed	No	Yes
BELOW (-1X)	Not meet or exit	Questionable	No	Yes or No

* Based on CEB analysis for certain knowledge workers, Recruiting Roundtable, *The Quality of Hire Imperative*, 2002; can be adjusted to specific organization experience or updated analysis

Figure 7.3 Defining Quality/Productivity Levels

© 2014 Human Capital Formation, LLC

One of the sources for the CEB case example was a study published by the *Journal of Applied Psychology*.[9] In this study, the researchers determined that output variability increased significantly with job complexity. An excerpt from the study conclusions makes the point succinctly on the challenges and benefits of measuring productivity (output):

> The data presented in this study show that individual differences in output are very large. It is clear that if people could be selected for jobs on the basis of a reliable measure of output, the differences in output between those selected and the average for the applicant pool would be very large...the employer must select on the basis of measures that have been shown to correlate with (and thus predict) future output.[10]

Once again, this indicates that a combination of performance, potential, advancement, and retention correlate to productivity (quality).

To demonstrate how our Weighted Quality Index (WQI) works, we use the hypothetical example of 25 people hired into Senior Researcher roles at a pharmaceutical company (see Figure 7.4). After 24 months, these researchers are evaluated based on performance, potential, promotion and retention. Based on this evaluation, the 25 are categorized by level of quality according to the Superstar, Star, Average, and Below levels. We then weight each by the corresponding productivity factor. A weighted average is calculated for the group by dividing the factor total by the number of individuals. This is the resulting WQI.

PRODUCT DEVELOPMENT SENIOR RESEARCH HIRES QUALITY ANALYSIS—LATEST 24 MONTHS AS OF DECEMBER 31, 2014

NAME	TITLE	DEPT	START	SOURCE	PRIOR CO/ DEPT	PERFORMANCE	POTENTIAL	PROMOTION	RETENTION	QUALITY RATING	FACTOR
Noma Vanhorn	Senior Researcher	2139	1/2/12	Referral	Honeywell	M	WP	N	Y	A	1
Marianela Abate	Senior Researcher	2574	1/13/12	Internal	Operations	E	P	N	Y	S	3
Steve Spratt	Senior Researcher	3140	2/22/12	Linkedin	P&G	M	WP	N	Y	A	1
Rodrigo Bonnie	Senior Researcher	3140	2/26/12	Linkedin	Raytheon	GE	H	Y	Y	SS	12
Sanford Gaccione	Senior Researcher	2574	3/21/12	Research	Cap Gemini	M	WP	N	Y	A	1
Jacquie Gandhi	Senior Researcher	3140	3/24/12	Internal	Operations	E	P	N	Y	S	3
Tiana Crutcher	Senior Researcher	2139	4/5/12	Linkedin	Booz Allen	M	WP	N	Y	A	1
Yuri Radigan	Senior Researcher	2139	5/2/12	Referral	Bristol Myers	E	P	N	Y	S	3
Cora Lapierre	Senior Researcher	3140	6/8/12	Agency	Merk & Co	M	WP	N	Y	A	1
Alicia Pledger	Senior Researcher	3140	6/15/12	Referral	P&G	M	WP	N	Y	A	1
Marybelle Dunnington	Senior Researcher	2574	7/21/12	Research	Sanifi	M	WP	N	Y	A	1
Annamarie Rux	Senior Researcher	3140	7/22/12	Referral	Eli-Lilly	M	WP	N	Y	A	1
Ross Rizer	Senior Researcher	3140	8/26/12	Internal	Marketing	E	P	N	Y	S	3
Dale Leffew	Senior Researcher	3140	8/30/12	Referral	P&G	GE	H	Y	Y	SS	12
Twana Pizzuto	Senior Researcher	2139	9/12/12	Internal	Quality Control	M	WP	N	Y	A	1
Kurtis Santillanes	Senior Researcher	3140	9/22/12	Internal	BPO	M	WP	N	Y	A	1
Epifania Pitt	Senior Researcher	2574	9/27/12	Rehire	Abbot	M	WP	N	Y	A	1
Beata Royal	Senior Researcher	2139	10/1/12	Research	Deloitte	M	WP	N	Y	A	1
Edison Shults	Senior Researcher	2139	10/2/12	Internal	Operations	E	P	N	Y	S	3
Phillip Makowski	Senior Researcher	2574	11/2/12	Referral	Booz Allen	M	WP	N	Y	A	1
James Brewer	Senior Researcher	2139	11/17/12	Research	Merk & Co	NM	Q	N	Y	B	-1
Beth Rodgers	Senior Researcher	3140	11/20/12	Referral	Bristol Myers	M	WP	N	Y	A	1
Greg Lutz	Senior Researcher	3140	12/13/12	Agency	Dyax	M	WP	N	Y	A	1
Rick Schlict	Senior Researcher	2574	12/20/12	Internal	Regulatory Affairs	E	P	N	Y	S	3
Helen Nomad	Senior Researcher	2139	12/28/12	Internal	Testing	E	H	N	N	B	-1
									FACTOR TOTAL		55
									WQI		-2.2

Figure 7.4 Weighted Quality Index (WQI) Demonstrated

As is apparent in the calculation of the WQI, the effect of the productivity factors is to increase the index disproportionately when Star talent or better is present. An organization could choose to use larger or, alternatively, more modest numerical factors for their quality levels and achieve a more or less exaggerated index. What is important is not the absolute value of the index, but rather how the index value compares to other time periods and how it is used to identify opportunities for improving talent quality.

As indicated in Figure 7.5, using the example of the 25 senior researchers, after "quality" is calculated, we can slice the data many ways, including by type—internal or external—and by source. The analytics are unlimited.

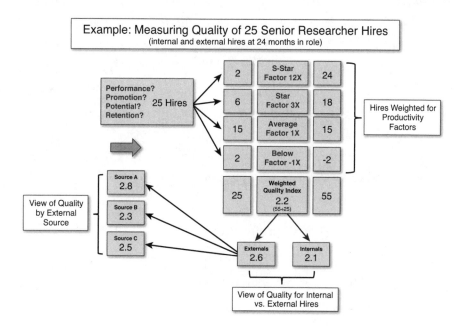

Figure 7.5 WQI Data Views

© 2014 Human Capital Formation, LLC

Naturally, the opportunity to begin measuring quality presents itself when a new hire is made, and for similar reasons the same opportunity exists when an internal placement is made. In the case of an internal move when an individual changes roles (not a promotion in place), an event is triggered that legitimately resets the counter for quality indicators. In effect, the organization makes a decision to fill a need with an internal resource or an external hire. A study conducted by the Corporate Executive Board captured variations in performance of internal transfers and reinforces the wisdom of measuring quality at this juncture. The study captured the frequency with which organizations say they were able to place an "A-level" internal hire (the right person for organization and job, with the right tools needed to do the job). Out of 38 organizations in the study, the best achieved A-level internal hires 18% of the time, and the worst only 1% of the time.[11] Especially for critical roles, it is essential to track quality of both internal and external hires.

Both outcomes can be tracked in the same way with comparable data using the WQI. The result is an index that expresses quality weighted for productivity in all roles being measured. The index can be broken down to the lowest component level (the individual) and sliced to provide any view desired for which corresponding data exists. For example

- Source of highest quality hires sorted by industry
- Quality of hire sorted by business unit
- Quality of internal versus external hires
- Quality of internal hires completing leadership program
- Quality of hire (total is current versus prior period)

Linda: Why do you think so many companies—including great ones—struggle to define and measure talent quality?

Tom: It is difficult to incrementally change from managing labor to managing knowledge workers—from a data, systems, skills, and philosophy standpoint. And it's probably impossible to do it in one fell swoop. The employment world has changed in so many ways over the last 35 years as we've evolved from a largely industrial economy to a largely knowledge-based one. Many leaders today started their careers at the tail end of the industrial world, and that is where they got their basic training. Therefore, it's hard for leaders to agree on the need to measure in this way when they haven't first recognized—and become aligned on—the meaning of this shift for their company.

We are only now realizing how important talent quality is to the value of a business. Next comes determining how to systematically measure and improve on it. This will be an evolving capability.

Technology and other new age industries have the best chance of getting there first because many don't carry the historical baggage of the way business used to work. They have been the first to tune into the quality imperative—which is no surprise given the intellectual capital they own and depend on.

The WQI itself should be calculated periodically (yearly, for example) using talent movement (hires and internal placements) after 24 months in a role. Because a numerical value is assigned to both performance and potential ratings and advancement and retention are "yes or no" factors, the ability to automate the computation of Hires/Placements by Quality Level from files storing this data is simplified. As Figure 7.6 shows, once a base year is established, future years can be compared to determine improvement or decline in the WQI. In this way, the WQI becomes the focal point for adjusting talent plans with the goal of increasing the index value.

	Calculate the Weighted Quality Index (WQI)								
	2010 Movement @ 24 months			2011 Movement @ 24 months			2012 Movement @ 24 months		
Quality Level	Hires/ Placements	Productivity Factor	Weighted Hires	Hires/ Placements	Productivity Factor	Weighted Hires	Hires/ Placements	Productivity Factor	Weighted Hires
SUPER STAR (12X)	2	12	24	7	12	84	9	12	108
STAR (3X)	22	3	66	38	3	114	42	3	126
AVERAGE (1X)	90	1	90	69	1	69	68	1	68
BELOW (-1X)*	6	-1	-6	4	-1	-4	4	-1	-4
Total	120		174	118		263	123		298
Quality Index		1.450			2.229			2.423	
Quality Index % Δ					54%			9%	
* Includes anyone who has exited the organization									

Figure 7.6 Calculating and Tracking WQI Performance
© 2014 Human Capital Formation, LLC

Linda: Practically speaking, all of this data comes from different sources in most organizations. Is it worth the amount of effort it would take to assemble this and update it regularly?

Tom: The cost of working around systems and data logistics issues is miniscule compared to the value of beginning to assemble this information and make good decisions that impact quality. Talent quality has a significant impact on the value of companies. In any industry, waiting would be an opportunity lost.

In addition, the systems to support this kind of reporting will evolve, and the logistics will become much more efficient over time. There is great value, though, in the absence of a single button to push, just working through the organizational change and creating new business routines that will enable visibility into such critical data.

The data underlying the WQI provides the ability to analyze talent activity from a number of vantage points. By doing so, organizations can evaluate which talent acquisition, development, or retention changes will be most likely to have a positive impact on the index. Figure 7.7 depicts how that analysis might impact the talent plan.

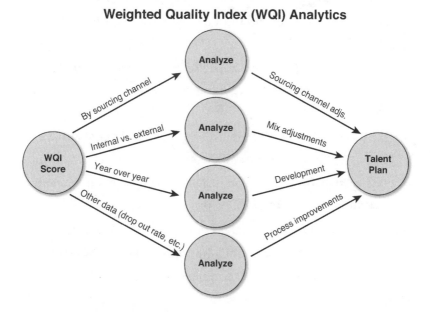

Figure 7.7 Driving Talent Plans with WQI Analytics

© 2014 Human Capital Formation, LLC

Talent quality has a direct impact on the creation and value of intellectual capital, often more than 50%—and sometimes higher than 90%—of the value of any corporation. Talent quality increases successful outcomes of business investments more than any other factor. Monitoring and adjusting talent investments in order to improve the WQI leads to positive returns on investment.

Endnotes

1. www.brainyquotes.com.

2. "Recruiting Roundtable, Realizing Breakthrough Gains in Recruiting Effectiveness," CEB, 2007.

3. *Topgrading*, Bradford D. Smart, Ph.D., Prentice Hall 1999.

4. Driving Quality Beyond the Point of Hire, Recruiting Roundtable, CEB, 2002.

5. *Chasing Stars: The Myth of Talent and the Portability of Performance*, Boris Groysberg, Princeton University Press 2010: 54.

6. HBR.org, "How Netflix Reinvented HR," Patty McCord, January-February 2014.

7. "What the Best Companies Do, Quality-Driven Executive Recruiting Function," CEB 2013.

8. "Driving Quality Beyond the Point of Hire," CEB, 2002.

9. "Individual Differences in Output Variability as a Function of Job Complexity," *Journal of Applied Psychology*, 1990.

10. Ibid.

11. "Identifying Drivers of Internal Transfer Performance, A Quantitative Analysis," CEB 2004

8

Attracting and Retaining the Human Capitalist Investor

- *What are "human capitalists?"*
- *Why do you want them in your organization?*
- *How can you attract and retain them?*
- *What role does employment branding play?*

Just as human capital is in effect considered "equity" to a corporation, the behavior of talent—or candidates—is more similar to that of an investor than a traditional applicant. The notion of "Organization Man" has given way to disruptors, innovators, and creators.

The label Organization Man described what was, beginning in the 1950s, the quintessence of work in America: an individual, almost always male, who ignored or buried his own identity and goals in the service of a large organization that rewarded his self-denial with a regular paycheck, the promise of job security, and a fixed place in the world.[1]

As articulated in Daniel Pink's *Free Agent Nation*, the Organization Man of the 1960s died an unheralded death during the 1980s and 1990s, in the wake of large corporations shedding hundreds of thousands of workers from their payrolls. It was the end of lifetime employment as we knew it. When Daniel Pink wrote his book in 2001, Manpower Inc. (a temp agency with more than 1,100 offices in the U.S.), had become the country's largest private employer.

Reid Hoffman, co-founder and Chairman of LinkedIn (arguably the twenty-first century's single most powerful tool for sourcing human capital) echoed Pink's comments: "There used to be a long-term pact between employee and employer that guaranteed lifetime employment in exchange for lifelong loyalty; this pact has been replaced by a performance-based, short-term contract that's perpetually up for renewal by both sides."[2] He points out that the loyalty of talent has shifted from their boss to their own network in his 2012 book, *The Start-Up of You*. This dynamic certainly makes sense from the perspective of a human capitalist.

Although there are no formal markets for human capital, clearly there are opportunities and buyers and sellers of talent. Financial markets are formal. In addition to buyers and sellers there are exchanges (NASDAQ, NYSE), and there are regulators such as the SEC. The role of regulators is distinct in financial markets, although regulatory structures already exist in markets regarding many aspects of company relations with employees. Interestingly, we see the foundation of human capital exchanges being formed. In combining LinkedIn and Glassdoor, you have both the means for access to human capitalist investors and valuation of the roles being offered. While not a formal human capital marketplace, the evolving structure does not appear to be so far from it.

Human capitalist investors think about employment the way financial investors think about buying stock. They expect a mix of "capital growth and dividend payout" consistent with their investment goals and risk tolerance.

"Capital growth" for the human capitalist means growth in those things that increase their capacity for generating future personal returns. There is an expectation of acquiring certain experience, knowledge, and skills as a result of their investment—that is, employment—decision. A track record of successfully "investing" in reputable companies also adds fuel to their growth potential.

"Dividend payout" for the human capitalist means economic reward in all forms including salary, short and long-term incentives, and benefits. Clearly for the human capitalist, dividend payout is baseline and must be competitive but will not often win the day on its own. The reason for this is quite rational.

For most of a human capitalist's career, "capital growth" has greater value than "dividend payout" because of its direct impact on future earnings potential. This impact can easily be multiple times current earnings. So the potential for acquiring knowledge, experience, and skills (and the risk of that not being so) weighs heavily on the employment decision and commitment of today's human capitalists.

This view of capital growth and dividend payout through the eyes of a human capitalist is consistent with a CEB case study in which the top attribute (out of 38) driving both attraction and commitment was "development opportunities," and the top attribute in driving attraction alone was "compensation."[3] In other words, "I need the right compensation to join, and I need the right development opportunities to join and to stay." Benefits, social responsibility, camaraderie, and a host of other important attributes did not measure up to these most important ones.

In contrast to the bygone prospect of lifetime employment and pension plans, the human capitalist is employed in a world designed for shorter-term horizons. The trappings of lifetime employment are gone, and today's human capitalist is more likely to "invest" with an expected horizon of three years in mind. In the past it was a red flag to see a resumé having 3 or 4 different employers within a 12–15 year period of time, but the opposite is true today. Today, a 12–15 year employment stint can carry with it a stigma of staleness and limited marketable knowledge.

This does not mean that today's relationship will only last three years, but it does mean that the human capitalist routinely reassesses their situation. This is not an announcement but rather a self-assessment of where they stand versus where they expected to be when their investment was initially made. Often, the first assessment occurs somewhere between the two- to three-year mark. What becomes visible are the decisions to pack it in and make a different investment. The decisions to reinvest are not necessarily visible even though they have been made. This same cycle is really no different from that of a financial investor, but it is less visible. Rest assured, every three years or so the human capitalist is likely to re-sign or resign.

These candidates consider alternative investments and compare the potential returns to those of their current investment. Different from the financial investor, to state the obvious, the human capitalist investor as a practical matter can only invest in one company at a time. Ultimately they make a decision to "invest," keeping in mind the timeframe they are willing to wait before seeing that investment bear fruit. At the end of the day, time is the constraint for this investor... their number of years are limited, so each one counts.

Like financial investors, the intent and strategies of human capitalist investors comes in a variety of flavors. You have your short-term and long-term investors, high yield (risk) and growth-oriented investors, and perhaps even an argument for day-traders. Which investors do you want? How do you attract and retain those investors? Like any corporation raising and retaining financial capital, it is important to have a clear view of who you are and what type of investor best fits your needs. There are countless products and services, case studies, and seminars hawking approaches to building employment branding and employment value propositions. In reality you need look no further than Investor Relations to find the best strategies for attracting and retaining critical talent.

Investor Relations leaders have put a fine point on persuading investors of the value inherent in trillions of dollars of securities as a means of capitalizing their businesses. It boils down to this:

1. Define the investor you want.

2. Define your investment offering.

3. Devise your campaign strategy.

4. Execute and measure outcomes.

Define the Investor You Want

With financial investors this analysis will range from location and size to risk profile and investment turnover rate. All of these attributes of the investor are important to be defined in great detail and should be driven by the longer-term capital needs and strategy of the business.

The correlation with human capitalist investors is nearly exact. What are the personal and career attributes and behaviors you are seeking? What length of commitment is ideal? What specialization and knowledge are required? There are multiple tools that need to work together internally to define the investor you want: company culture, proprietary competency models, job profiles, and so on. Any and all such tools must be developed and orchestrated to clearly define the human capitalist investor profile you want, particularly those for critical roles.

Define Your Investment Offering

Of the investors who fit your profile, which would likely profit the most from investing in your company (that is, a win-win)? How do you know? How do they know? This is where positioning becomes important. It begins, of course, by defining your company's investment advantages. Those advantages are ultimately presented in a multitude of ways to your potential investors. This is where you make an important choice.

Many employment brands and messages attempt to be all things to everyone. They are broad and nebulous and feature predictable images of a diverse cast of characters. A few effectively hone in on the real target (think about the Marines' campaign targeting potential recruits). Most of them land somewhere in the vast in-between.

The employment brand message should be directed at the heart of the talent most essential to your organization. This laser-beam approach (described in detail later in this chapter) accomplishes several things:

- Attracts and retains the most critical talent
- Results in targeted brand promises that have a better chance of being kept
- Has a halo effect on the rest of the organization
- Can be easily adjusted for a broader reach

Linda: Tom, I'm not sure I buy the "halo effect" of an employment brand that is designed to attract only the critical talent for an organization. The downside is that you'll miss most of the existing organization and its potential candidates with your messaging. Sounds to me like you're ignoring everyone else. I can just imagine what the CFO will say when the employment brand is focused only on engineers. Your halo sounds a little bit like vapor to me!

Tom: Remember that this employment brand positioning is designed to attract "the critical talent" not "only the critical talent." There is a big difference. It is highly likely that a well-constructed position designed to attract talent to roles deemed critical will succeed in attracting talent to noncritical roles as well. The standard should be messaging that would be neutral or better for noncore talent.

There are plenty of brand benefits that are "cost of entry" and will be present and speak equally to all audiences. To be competitive, however, a strong brand position has to lead with significant points of leverage that are targeted and can be protected from encroachment. Putting this sharp of a point on the instrument is not likely when targeting to the entire organization. You must narrow the field to the most critical talent.

The reason the "halo" effect works is because focusing on and securing top quality critical talent benefits everyone through the business stability it creates, and that fact becomes obvious. In the CEB study entitled "Organization Stability and Growth Rate," for example, are attributes that communicate stability and future opportunity that rate highly with all talent in terms of attraction and retention. The organization at large understands intuitively which core talent makes or breaks the business, and acknowledging and acting on these facts in a way that is respectful of everyone is a good thing. That's what creates the halo.

Linda: Ok, sounds like a reasonable theory. So, everyone is happy if they see that the talent in critical roles is in good shape. It indirectly provides job security, organizational growth, and, in turn, more career opportunities for all. There must be a downside when the opposite occurs, correct?

Tom: I am willing to bet that when the accounting, HR, or legal teams at Coca-Cola see key marketing people jumping ship, they get nervous. The marketing people at KPMG get nervous when they see key audit and tax partners jump ship. Everyone else gets nervous when they see engineers at Raytheon or top researchers at Merck & Co. leaving.

All talent that is right for an organization respond to a message that hits the strategic bull's-eye regardless of what role they are being asked to play. The benefits are intuitive.

The employment brand is the means by which companies sell their employment opportunity to the talent—the investors—that they want. The brand position has to be more fact-based than aspirational. It has to be true, it has to be appealing enough, and it has to express why you are a different and better choice over your competition. The employment brand is a promise that is communicated through every point of contact with potential and existing talent. It extends throughout the employment lifecycle. Your talent will expect you to deliver on these brand promises; over-promising and under-delivering will result in more than just bad PR (compare Glassdoor's lowest rated employers list with their employment brands for vivid examples).

Devise Your Campaign Strategy

The campaign strategy brings together your target market, positioning, company information, and various marketing tools and how they work in conjunction with one another. The campaign communicates the investment advantages that are most important to the talent you want throughout the entire employment lifecycle and beyond. Think investor relations: There is an Investor Relations department, and though they do the heavy and continuous lifting, many other departments assist in the effort (Corporate Communications, for example) to sell the company. Most corporations have employees who could do a pretty good job of articulating the main reasons for buying their stock.

The talent equivalent of Investor Relations in most organizations is embedded in Talent Management. Talent Management has to execute branding in the same way as the investor relations function. The campaign must be pervasive to be effective, particularly on delivering the brand promise.

Linda: What do you mean by the brand campaign stretching beyond the employment life cycle? Sounds like an alumni program, right? Honestly, in a world where employment has changed to a lifecycle of 3 years rather than 30, I question the value of investing resources that way. How do you reconcile all that with the shorter-term nature of commitments that these "investors" make?

Tom: "Beyond" can be at the end of three or four or five years if a highly valued person leaves the organization for an opportunity with another company. Thirty years ago at Coca-Cola we said "good riddance" to that person. They were ostracized. Now they are a primary source of talent, and that is true with virtually every company with which I've consulted. I advocate communicating with critical talent whether they are inside or outside of the company. Why wouldn't I rehire great talent two or three times during their careers if it were mutually beneficial? Great investor and great investment.

Linda: Wait a minute, what happened to all the discipline around defining the investor you want? It sounds like you are just reacting to whatever an individual decides to do?

Tom: That's a good point. Most human capitalist investors make a conscious decision every three years or so to stay at or change organizations. They make a decision to re-sign or resign. Ideally, both your employment brand position and the immediate opportunity for that talent are strong enough to drive a decision to reinvest, but that's not always true. I have experienced multiple occasions where a top talent had an opportunity outside the company that was simply better for their career at that point in time. It was a better career choice to move; a few years later we got them back, stronger than if they had stayed with us instead.

The stars don't align 100% of the time internally, so you often have to allow for that in order to flex and innovate and grow.

On the other hand, some companies are not built to rehire. Some strategically fuel their organizations directly and uniquely with early career hires (straight out of college) and have structures that don't easily accommodate rehires and mid-career external hires. It takes scale and discipline to make that structure work, but if that is their model and it is successful, then their definition of the investor they want will be different than many others.

The typical investor relations function communicates with investors and potential investors throughout the investor life cycle using multiple media platforms:

- Press releases
- Website
- Blogs and social media
- Annual reports
- Shareholder letter
- Press kits
- Roadshows
- Conferences
- Analyst and investor days
- Conference calls

Most of these investor relations platforms have equal potential as part of a campaign strategy to attract and retain human capitalist investors as well.

Execute and Measure Outcomes

Strategy is just a buzzword if you can't execute. You've defined the investor you want, the position that highlights the strongest points of your company's offering, and designed a holistic campaign. Execution requires orchestrating all of the touch points across the employment life cycle by educating and enlisting all of the stakeholders. Ultimately, the measure of success brings us back to movement in the Weighted Quality Index (WQI), although there are subprocess measures that apply to this specific area as well, such as

- Perception studies:
  - Internal surveys (employee engagement, candidate experience, and so on)
  - Participative surveys (CEB, for example)
  - Independent surveys (Glassdoor)
  - Awards and recognition (Great Place to Work)
  - Strategic turnover analysis-expectations, trends, reasons

Human capitalist investors in critical roles have to be rerecruited periodically throughout their tenure. By definition, these are an organization's most highly valued human assets and a competitor's most sought-after prospects.

Laser Approach to Creating the Employment Brand Position

Why are efforts to brand employment missing the mark so often today, and how can they be sharpened and effectively directed to the most critical talent? The answer to this question is strategy—or lack thereof. By the time most organizations scribe an Employee Value

Proposition, it resembles a buffet of HR jargon, and getting to a tagline is the only relief.

Consider this sampling of recent employment taglines in the marketplace:

"Help Make Dreams Real"

"Join the Revolution"

"360° Energy"

"Passionate About People"

"Run with the Best"

"Success So Big, You Can Taste It"

"Careers for a Global Generation"

Based on reading them alone, we don't know if these taglines are effective, but the more generic the tagline, the less likely it is to target a certain population and inspire action. To develop a strong brand position, these questions have to be answered:

- Have I defined my target audience—my human capitalist investor?

- Have I identified the investment advantages I own that are most important to that target audience?

- How do our investment advantages differentiate us from the competition?

This last point is fundamental and often missed. Positioning a brand is done for the sole purpose of competing; therefore, you must address the competition to develop an effective space for your brand.

The sequence of work to create and deliver a competitive and targeted brand message is

- **Strategize**—Determine key brand equities and develop brand position

- **Translate**—Develop the brief
- **Create**—Create the advertising (including tagline)

Companies often head to the ad agency without having done the strategic work first. The result is an unguided, ineffective tagline or logo and tens of thousands of dollars wasted with unintended market consequences that may leave the company worse off. Advertising conveys a brand and its promises. False advertising is always worse than no advertising at all.

The cornerstone of a strong brand position is a few essential and meaningful differences. The temptation to create a list of brand attributes that resembles a buffet must be resisted. An adage used among brand marketers reinforces this point: "If you throw six tennis balls at someone, chances are he will miss all of them. If you throw one, chances are he will catch it."

The branding question is, "What do I have that is important to who I want?" In fact, one option is simply asking those people and getting their feedback. So assuming the target investor has been well-defined, you find a representative sample and gather information from them. These are people who may already be in your organization as well as externals who match the definition. Sources of input from those investors can include

- Surveys
- Exit interviews
- Recruiter assessments
- Candidate and employee feedback
- Focus groups
- Quantitative research

Importantly, the data you are evaluating should pertain to talent for critical roles that closely match your definition of the ideal investor.

It is important to recognize that all 38 employment attributes from the CEB study are valid to some degree and many are even "cost of entry" attributes—you won't get further consideration without them. Let's assume your target audience told you these attributes are the most important to them:

- Market position
- Career opportunity
- Organization size and scope
- Senior leadership reputation
- Compensation
- Retirement benefits
- Innovation
- Social responsibility
- Brand awareness
- Work-life-balance

The next stage is where the real leverage to brand positioning comes into play. You have come up with ten attributes that are valid for your company and most important to your target audience. Next, identify your true brand equities by doing two things:

1. Evaluate how you actually perform in delivering these investment advantages.

2. Evaluate how your performance in delivering these investment advantages compares to your primary competitors.

As the matrix in Figure 8.1 shows, there are four outcome categories (and consequences) of these evaluations, as discussed in the following sections.

Figure 8.1 Determining Employment Brand Equities
© 2014 Human Capital Formation, LLC

Potential Vulnerabilities

This category reflects the same low performance by both you and your competition. Although you are judged to be at parity with the competition, you are vulnerable to improvements they choose to make in this important area.

Potential Strengths

Your performance is also not high against attributes in this category, but you outperform the competition. These are potential strengths that can add to the brand and motivate investors while being further strengthened with attention over time.

Equivalent Equities

This category reflects your strong performance while being at parity with the competition. These are attributes that can support the brand position but do not create competitive advantage.

Key Brand Equities

This category reflects strong performance that is significantly higher than the competition. These are the attributes that have the ability to differentiate you in a way that is meaningful to your target audience while being difficult for your competition to encroach upon. Key brand equities are the backbone of your employment brand.

After this work has been completed, a strong employment brand positioning statement can be crafted that summarizes the proposition. A brand positioning statement describes who the brand is for, what its key advantages are, compelling reasons to believe them, and the competitive frame of reference.

Last, communication specialists (ad agencies, public relations, and so on) create attractive messaging by providing them with a clear description of our communication objectives and employment branding. The brief to the agency should include

- The employment brand and attributes
- The reason advertising is needed (brand perception, awareness, familiarity, and so on)
- Who the brand is competing with
- Who you are targeting advertising toward (such as investors for critical roles!)
- The one key idea you want your ad to convey
- What favorable change you expect in the target's attitude (that is, what to measure)

With this kind of laser approach, employment branding becomes strategic to attracting and retaining the right critical talent.

"The strategy has to come first because the strategy is what determines the tactics that you need. If you have decided to go from New York to Washington by train, you wouldn't call a taxi to take you to the airport."[4]

Endnotes

1. *Free Agent Nation,* Daniel H. Pink, Warner Books 2001.

2. *The Start-up of You*, Reid Hoffman and Ben Casnocha, Crown Business 2012.

3. "Attracting and Retaining Critical Talent Segments: Identifying Drivers of Attraction and Commitment in the Global Labor Market," CEB, 2006

4. *The End of Marketing As We Know It*, Sergio Zyman, Harper-Collins 1999.

9

Looking Back and Looking Forward

During the lifetime of most senior business leaders in place today, the world has moved from the Industrial into the Post-Industrial age, one where knowledge has become the means of production. As recently as 1980, market values of public companies were still roughly equivalent to book values. During the ensuing 20 years, patent applications soared, and grants by the U.S. patent office tripled after having been flat for the previous 15 years. This, along with business activity that grew many other forms of intellectual capital, created a 75% difference between market and book values for the average public company, reflecting the value of these unrecorded intangible assets (see discussion of accounting limitations in Chapters 2, "Is Your Most Important Asset Really an Asset?," and 3, "Valuing and Evaluating Companies and Their Intellectual Capital").

The Dow Jones Industrial Average, a barometer of industrial evolution, inducted the first information technology company in 1979, when IBM replaced Chrysler. In that same year, pharmaceutical giant Merck replaced Esmark Steel. During the next 20 years, companies heavy in intellectual capital such as American Express, Coca-Cola, Hewlett-Packard, Walt Disney, Boeing, Microsoft, and Intel replaced companies such as Johns-Manville, Owens-Illinois, U.S. Steel, Westinghouse, International Harvester, Goodyear Tire & Rubber, and

Bethlehem Steel. The market's investment dollars tilted unmistakably toward the value of intellectual capital.

Many successful industrial age corporations took a back seat to companies that greatly benefited from value created by knowledge, accumulating intellectual capital that drove huge market valuations. And those same industrial age corporations had leapt over commodity-centered entities that ruled the market 50 years earlier (such as American Smelting, American Sugar, Corn Products Refining, and International Nickel). Every period of succession reflects change in economic value, and the one we are in the midst of is arguably the most profound.

The primary means by which value is created has changed, and the role of people in the value chain has changed along with it. In the past, labor has served machines in creating value. Today, machines serve knowledge workers in creating value. This is not incremental change; it is an entirely different model. Understandably, the management consequences of this seismic shift are still not fully comprehended, much less attended to.

Although many modern human resource functional initiatives (organization effectiveness, leadership development, succession planning, and so on) seem to make sense given the new role of people, they are not linked to business consequences. Because the underlying model of value creation—as it relates to these initiatives—has not been considered, incremental actions are taken out of business context. Results are therefore not measured in a way that is relevant—or even understandable—to other parts of the business. The rest of the organization senses this, and skepticism prevents HR from influencing others, driving meaningful change, and ultimately, earning that elusive "seat at the table."

Continuing to make things *better* instead of *different* won't be good enough.

Consider three examples:

- Developing managers
- Improving work/life balance
- Improving pay fairness

In the future, to align deployment of knowledge workers with the creation of market value, things must be different, not just better. The following sections describe how these examples of HR challenges might be addressed differently.

Manager as Knowledge Conductor

In the creation of intellectual capital, everyone is a knowledge worker. The capability that a manager must have is "organizing knowledge effectively" by bringing knowledge from many sources together to produce the desired outcome. Those sources are ultimately people, whether employed or contracted, present or remote. What is the most effective way to organize the efforts of people developing and patenting complex medical or engineering solutions? What are the most critical factors for success? How can expectations for everyone involved be clearly set? What are the barriers and how can they be removed? How can learning be institutionalized? How are results measured? What learning can be reapplied?

Without a doubt, the responsibility of managing people sits squarely on the shoulders of their managers. To quote Peter Drucker, "The right definition of a manager is one who is responsible for the application and performance of knowledge."[1] Yet when managers do an ineffective job—as evidenced by attrition, employee complaints, poor results, and so on—it's often tossed over the fence to HR to "fix it."

It is difficult to find good examples of training—or "leadership development"—practices, tools, or processes that are geared to this newly-evolved role: managers who must channel knowledge from knowledge workers into valuable intellectual property. Although an entire industry has mushroomed around "leadership development," little of what is seen in practice boils down to the role of managing the productivity of knowledge workers. Much of the content is focused on managing up—influencing, strategic planning, and so on—and managing down in a traditional sense—delegating, interviewing, conducting performance appraisals.

Transforming managers from bosses to knowledge conductors is a high-return activity and demands innovation, investment, and careful application.

Linda: Don't knowledge managers also need to hire, train, and manage performance? All that work doesn't go away, does it?

Tom: No, it doesn't go away; it is arguably more important now than ever, but it has to be done differently. Knowledge workers are literally the means of production—knowledge managers have asset responsibility for these workers in the broadest terms.

The knowledge manager's role of applying knowledge to knowledge (broadly speaking, performance management) amounts to "activating" these assets, while the manager's role in hiring and development denotes asset stewardship.

The knowledge manager is clearly the buyer and closer in hiring transactions. While other experts can hopefully be relied on to source and pre-sell talent on a given opportunity, the knowledge manager is the decision maker. Also the knowledge worker wants to be seen and treated as an "asset" rather than a "cost." It is the knowledge manager's responsibility to impart this attitude on behalf of the company, and it begins with hiring.

The same holds true for training and development. These activities are strategic to asset stewardship and to knowledge worker engagement and performance. As with hiring, managers can often rely on subject matter experts to execute agreed upon plans, but the ultimate responsibility remains theirs.

Managing performance is the focal point of knowledge management. Different from manual labor, in knowledge work the task is not a given. Productivity is dependent on a manager clearly specifying the required result. The knowledge worker must determine the task, a step that may include the manager in a coaching or advisory capacity.

Orchestrating the mix and efforts of multiple knowledge workers to achieve a particular result is the mega skill of a knowledge manager; literally, the same skill required of a symphony orchestra conductor.

Importantly, knowledge managers must also ensure that knowledge workers teach what they learn to others. This new dimension to performance management, let's call it "asset proliferation," unlocks the potential for exponential growth in a knowledge economy.

Enabling Results Based Work

With knowledge workers, attempts to improve personal flexibility (typically led by HR) by balancing "time doing tasks" with "time not doing tasks," does not solve the issue. Knowledge work is results-oriented rather than task- or time-driven.

F.W. Taylor, the mechanical engineer who famously sought to optimize work in the industrial age with his "scientific management" approach, emphasized enforced standards for all tasks. When Taylor started to study the shoveling of sand, he could take it for granted that the sand had to be shoveled.[2] Such is the case with the task of making and moving things. But knowledge work is quite the opposite.

In knowledge work the task is not given—it has to be determined. To do so, expected results must be clearly specified. Following this, knowledge work is not physically observed like shoveling sand, and it isn't constrained in the same way by time and space. The task of the knowledge worker is a function of knowledge rather than simply time.

Because of this dynamic, there is flexibility available to the knowledge worker that was not available to the sand shoveler. When and where work is performed is not crucial. Judging capacity and specifying expected results *is* crucial, as is the skill of managers (knowledge conductors) at doing so.

Redefining and supporting the nature of results-based work is the best way to improve the personal flexibility of knowledge workers. Two levers to doing this are

- Enhancing managers' skill at articulating expected work results and planning for capacity
- Focusing on flexible work locations more so than time

Often discussions on such topics are governed by the HR team, which is focused on compliance, liability, and consistent application of rules (understandably, given their typical role). It's not easy, then, to create entirely new environments and frameworks specifically for knowledge workers. This must change.

Value-Based Compensation

It is a sad truth to say that HR has a better chance of being rewarded for decreasing the cost of people while revenue remains flat, than for increasing the cost of people while revenue also increases, at an even greater rate. Even in a knowledge economy, people as a resource are by default commoditized through HR practices at most companies. From market surveys that result in pegging a 2.5% merit pool, to shaving the salary targets from the 84th to the 82nd percentile, HR is routinely rewarded for cutting the cost of people, while doing so fairly. That view of compensation is one of cost control rather than value creation.

What if that were not the case? We know that certain talent in every organization produces much more value, by design, than others. Not because they are better people, but because the industry and roles they are in and the work they do result in that outcome. But market survey information does not do a good enough job of differentiating the value of a brand director at a consumer products company from one at a bank, for example. The components of intellectual capital that drive market values at those two institutions do differentiate them, however. Designing compensation strategies to more closely fit the relative value of roles in companies, based on the value they create, would shift the financial view of people from one of cost to one of investment.

In this scenario the categories themselves would be valued according to their contribution to market value of the company (through the intellectual capital they are associated with) rather than external benchmarks that are too often irrelevant. If human capital is indeed the new means of production, we will need data and information systems that can guide this type of optimization.

Looking Forward

Many of the largest companies are evolving from the industrial age while adding value incrementally in the form of intellectual capital produced by their knowledge workers. It has been difficult for most, in this changing environment, to put a finger on critical sources of value, much less take action to drive productivity. In the future, companies will need the equivalent of financial infrastructures that currently enable the management of tangible capital and assets. All of the same discipline that is wrapped up in planning, accounting, analyzing, maintaining, tracking, and auditing for tangible resources will need to be applied to intangible resources and their production.

The need exists now, although a change of this magnitude will certainly be difficult to easily justify and undertake for companies evolving from industrial age environments. It is much easier to isolate the pressing need when you consider brand new industries such as biotechnology. Biotech companies are nearly a pure play in intellectual capital. Non-existent before the mid 1970s, the curve in patents filed by new biotech firms was almost straight up beginning in 1980 before tapering to current high levels in the late 1990s, and their market valuations show it. Amgen is a good example (Figure 3.3, Chapter 3). Born in 1980, the company had an enterprise value of nearly $100 billion by 2012, with 93% of that value in intellectual capital. The critical talent for these firms was conscripted largely from research universities, which remain important partners and ongoing sources of talent. Without these scientists, biotech firms would have no intellectual capital and no products. Yet, as of today there is little innovation to accounting and financial infrastructure to measure and manage their essential intangible assets.

Will infrastructure (process, procedures, systems, and so on) similar to that brought to bear on managing financial capital ever really exist for human and intellectual capital? How will that capability evolve?

As was the case for existing financial infrastructure, two primary business forces will drive the outcome:

- **Internal Forces**

  Management requires relevant information to make business decisions. Financial information became increasingly important for this reason during the Industrial Age, with accounting initially born as a profession in the late 1800s in England and the U.S. As demonstrated in this book, a new need for relevant information has evolved as human and intellectual capital have taken center stage in creating market value.

- **External Forces**

  Investors require relevant information to make investment decisions. The Securities and Exchange Commission (SEC) was formed in 1934 to protect investors and issue regulations to achieve this. In 2001 the Financial Accounting Standards Board (FASB), the body that codifies accounting regulations that are subsequently enforced by the SEC, proposed adding a project to its research agenda named *Disclosure of Information About Intangible Assets Not Recognized in Financial Statements.* This proposal reflected a clear understanding of the need, if not the solution, to provide investors with information relevant to intellectual capital value and its creation. The status of this proposal is discussed in the next pages.

Financial accounting and infrastructure initially grew up inside companies as a result of internal forces, followed years later by external regulatory efforts aimed at informing and protecting investors. It remains to be seen which force will drive the initial effort to formalize infrastructure for managing human and intellectual capital and which will follow.

Internally, CEOs appear to have an intuitive sense that talent strategies, the engine for intellectual capital, must be changed. Price Waterhouse Cooper's 2014 CEO Survey, canvassing more than 1,300 CEOs in 68 countries, found that 93% recognize the need to change their talent strategies, although most do not know where to begin. Nor, the study tells us, do most CEOs believe HR is ready for the task.[3]

On the positive side, technologies on the market that are able to provide a foundation for the new work infrastructure look very promising. Solutions from newcomer Workday, a creator of HR and financial enterprise cloud applications, would appear to provide the elements necessary to do the work envisioned. The Workday Human Capital Management application includes Project and Work Management designed to enable organizations to create, manage, and track initiatives; build project plans; and utilize project breakdown structures that include phases, tasks, and milestones. Together with integrative and data analytics capabilities, systems like Workday's appear to offer the kind of capability needed to follow and manage the production of intellectual capital all the way from critical talent to work processes and critical success factors.

External forces that drive change in what businesses communicate to shareholders and other stakeholders include, but are not limited to, the SEC and FASB. While the SEC is a U.S. government agency, it recognizes and hence relies on pronouncements of the FASB (a professional organization) as being "authoritative" regarding accounting principles and standards. Based on a report written by a former FASB staff member on challenges in the "new economy," the FASB circulated a research project proposal, *Disclosure of Information About Intangible Assets Not Recognized in Financial Statements*, to stakeholders for their comments in August 2001.

The stated goals of the proposal were

- Make new information vital to well-reasoned investment decisions available to investors
- Take a first step in what might become an evolution toward recognition in an entity's financial statements of internally generated intangible assets

Interestingly, one of several related factors considered but not included in the FASB's scope at that time was information on employee turnover. In the underlying discussion, the people connection to intellectual capital was clearly recognized by the proposal's authors.

The proposal was circulated to stakeholders (major corporations, professional organizations, accounting firms) for comment, as is customary, and they received 61 responses, generally in favor of the proposal. We include two examples of responses in the Appendix that effectively convey the discussion happening at that time (AFL-CIO and American Accounting Association). The response from the Director, Office of Investment of the AFL-CIO, was particularly insightful. AFL-CIO member pension funds held over $3.5 trillion in assets providing retirement security to union members at the time. The response expressed well-founded interest in investors having access to all the relevant information to manage these investment funds.

The AFL-CIO letter commented succinctly on the growing gap between book assets and real value-creating assets (including brands and human capital) and recommended, "measures of intellectual capital preservation and development in setting executive pay."

But then, out of the blue, came October 2001 and Enron. One of the largest public accounting firms disappeared. On the heels of the Sarbanes-Oxley Act of 2002, the focus of the public accounting world and the SEC shifted and fixated on internal controls. I personally spent an entire year just implementing the extensive SOX control requirements as a public company CFO in 2003. Enron changed the mood in the accounting and public company regulatory realm and shifted agendas, including at the FASB. Understandably, SOX was conservative in nature—new age accounting for intellectual capital was not.

In the ensuing years the FASB focused on, among other things, a major effort to normalize accounting standards around the world through participation as a leader and partner with international standard setters in designing International Financial Reporting Standards (IFRS).

At about the same time as the FASB proposal and Enron in 2001, the Global Reporting Initiative (GRI) was born. The GRI quickly became the new standard setter for reporting on corporate global sustainability efforts. The undertaking by corporations to comply with the GRI framework has been significant, and the benefits of such an endeavor are self-evident.

As you can see, the issue of disclosing intangible assets not reported on financial statements unexpectedly took a back seat to a number of other mega-issues impacting the accounting and business world at the time.

What can we expect from the FASB and SEC in the future? The 2001 proposal was inactive and officially removed from the FASB research agenda in 2004. On the periphery, some of the issues raised in the proposal were at least considered during follow-on work related to existing standards for recording intangible assets that are acquired outright or through business combinations. In the ten years since the proposal was removed, however, trillions of dollars in additional intellectual capital has been created and paid for by investors but still not recorded on companies' books. The gap continues to widen, and the issues will not disappear. Sooner or later, the same considerations that put intangible assets on the FASB 2001 research agenda will prevail, with even more urgency, due to accelerating materiality.

Let's assume for this discussion that accounting for internally developed intangible assets is finally addressed by the FASB at some future date. It would be normal course for implementation of any new reporting standards to begin with disclosures of intellectual capital, likely in the footnotes to financial statements, and later evolve to include actual values recorded in the financial statements. Again, because human capital is the only source of intellectual capital, the work would eventually center on this aspect.

What types of things will investors need to know about the active component of IC, human capital, to make well-reasoned investment decisions? Based on a review of the report that spurred the original FASB proposal and on proprietary analysis, I believe investors would want to understand specific information about critical roles, including:

- Description of critical role categories
- Main strategies for supplying human capital
- Capacity analytics (future focused)
- Tenure analytics
- Demographic analytics
- Mix of permanent and contingent human capital
- Analysis of human capital quality and trends
- Analysis of human capital productivity
- Important practices and policies (development, compensation, and so on)
- General organization stability—strategies and key metrics for the supporting roles (noncritical)
- % Headcount/payroll for critical vs. supporting roles
- Material changes in human capital practices or systems
- Audit report

Eventually, business information capabilities will evolve to meet the needs of management and investors, driven by economics, just as all our financial systems have evolved up until today. The economics of intellectual capital and value creation are widely acknowledged, and now it is only a matter of when rather than if.

Will internal forces lead as they did in developing financial infrastructure, or will they follow external forces, whatever those may be?

All firms will ultimately benefit from the future infrastructure and systems that will support managing their primary means of value creation. Performance management systems, recruiting systems, and other current HR systems have served a useful purpose. But they aren't enough to rest 93% of the market value in a biotechnology firm upon, or even 85% of a consumer products firm, or 65% of a retailer—can anyone afford not to manage the majority of their market value? I think not, but the question remains, "Who is going to lead this change?"

The "who" is the single biggest gap. Who will provide the leadership required for designing and implementing new business routines that respond to the CEOs' intuition and take advantage of emerging technologies? Who will initiate the identification and connection of critical roles with intellectual capital? Who will track and correlate talent quality with IC production and growth in market value?

Most CEOs believe Finance is prepared to capitalize on transformative global trends in their area; most believe HR is not.[4] Could the answer be somewhere in between—a hybrid function that currently doesn't exist?

Endnotes

1. *Post Capitalist Society*, Peter F. Drucker, HarperBusiness 1993.

2. Ibid.

3. 17th Annual Global CEO Survey: The Talent Challenge, www.pwc.com

4. Ibid.

10

Who Is Responsible?
What Is the Purpose of HR?

- *Where we've been*
- *Where we are now*
- *Where we need to go*
- *What good looks like*

Back in 2001, Apple introduced the iPod and proclaimed that for the first time, you could carry your entire music library in your pocket and listen to it wherever you go. At that time, portable music players weren't new—11 years earlier, Sony introduced the Walkman, and then many other makes and models followed. But none were as portable or held as much music (5GB of music—1,000 songs in your pocket!) as the iPod. Although anyone could use a Walkman to listen to music on the go, they were forced to lug around cassette tapes or, later, CDs and listen to albums largely in the same sequence in which they were originally produced.[1]

Initially, the iPod was scorned by some: Who would need to have that much music so close at hand? What purpose does it serve? How can you listen to all that music at one time? Some naysayers kept a tight grip on their Walkmans and cassette tapes even years later, as if to prove a point.

Turns out, there were a lot of people who wanted their music—all of it—close at hand. There were other unexpected and positive consequences of the iPod for consumers too, such as the easy iTunes music management software, the ability to buy music instantly—particularly single songs, and the shuffle feature, which allowed users to listen to random selections without regard to the intent of the music's producers. Apple's ability then and now to tap into what consumers want before they even know they want it is stuff of legends.

So what will it be for HR—iPod or Walkman? Everything we see tells us the world needs the HR equivalent of an iPod. Peoples' roles in creating value have been altered dramatically without a correspondingly dramatic shift in HR's understanding of and approach to these new relationships.

HR transformation so far amounts to an upgrade from cassette to CD, but still using a Walkman. Between iPod and obsolescence, what factors will determine HR's future in supporting business needs in a world of value created by knowledge workers?

Where We've Been

The roots of HR as we know it today grew out of legitimate and worthy needs during the time of the Second World War—protecting workers and managing necessary administrative tasks related to payroll and work schedules. Additional requirements arose over time with labor and employment laws, and as companies realized the importance of hiring and training. Innovations came about over time related to benefits administration, performance management, interviewing, and training, and they were managed by what became known as the Personnel Department. In most organizations, this team worked in a tactical, reactive way, tracking far behind the pace of business leaders who were setting and implementing the strategy for growth. From "Personnel" grew the notion of "Human Resources," which was transformative in its heyday. The idea that corporations would focus more on what mattered to employees was inventive at the time. Over time, more changes took place within the world of HR, as recruiting morphed into "talent acquisition" and performance management into "talent management."

In fact, the history of HR reveals a wrestling match over functional transformation that has lasted for decades now. Business has been attempting to "transform" HR since the conceptualization of that post-personnel people department in the mid-1960s.

Unknown to many current HR practitioners, the term "HR transformation" actually was coined in the late 1980s; it wasn't until the 2000s, however, that it caught on in a significant way and became the absolute HR rage.

So what exactly did HR transformation mean? The classic David Ulrich model is worth revisiting.[2] Ulrich inspired a generation of HR business partners focused on delivering more strategic outcomes and business unit-aligned support. Then, in his 2009 book *HR Transformation*, Ulrich refined his model and the meaning of HR transformation with a four-element roadmap:

> **Element 1**—Why? HR transformation leaders must first ask, "Why are we transforming HR?" Transformation takes place as a response to a business context and set of conditions. Context has specific stakeholders. These general conditions and stakeholders give us the rationale as to why we should transform HR.
>
> **Element 2**—So what? What will we get from HR transformation? Leaders define explicit benefits and measurable outcomes—typically tied to the capabilities that an organization requires to successfully adapt and compete.

Element 3—How do we transform? To achieve the results outlined in element two, a new approach to HR skills, process, technology and practices is typically needed.

Element 4—Who does what? What newly defined roles, responsibilities, and measures of success will ensure transformation?

Ulrich adamantly distinguishes this holistic concept from the idea of pulling a single best practice out of an organization and trying to transform around it:

> As we talk about transforming HR, one of the mistakes that often happens is we do one little thing, and we assume it's an HR transformation. Companies love what's called best practices. So if a company is doing 8 or 9 different things, we take one and we say, "We've stolen their best practice," and it's implemented and it's worked. Here's a lesson learned, it's not true. A best practice from a company doesn't work, what you need is a best system.

From Ulrich's work grew a new and popular HR structure—familiar to many large businesses today. The trends around organizational structure, roles, and responsibilities in recent years have been

- **Shared Services**—Centralized teams of (sometimes outsourced) HR professionals tasked with handling routine requests, complaints, or questions. These typically include payroll issues, employee relations, and benefits administration. Note that this work used to represent the lion's share of old school HR generalist work; now—for many remaining in such roles—this work has all but vanished.

- **Centers of Excellence**—More specialized and seasoned teams of HR professionals with deep expertise in a particular area, responsible for building enterprise-wide processes and tools to drive sustainable, scalable HR results. These areas typically include Talent Acquisition, Talent Management, Learning, Compensation, Benefits, and so on.

- **HR Business Partners**—Strategic HR generalists assigned to senior business leaders throughout the organization to act as talent advisors. They partner with these leaders to plan and implement talent solutions that drive business results. They liaise between Shared Services, Centers of Excellence, and their business group to add relevance and value.

Dramatically improved technology supported this organizational design transformation. Oracle, Workday, IBM, and PeopleSoft all acquired or developed robust human capital technology during this time, which aided the implementation of the newly "transformed" HR model.

At the same time, organizations have grown leaner, with fewer front-line and mid-level managerial positions than ever. There are broader spans of control, more direct reports, matrixed responsibilities, and differentiated workforces (contractors, virtual employees, part-timers). All this, of course, during unprecedented and rapidly changing business and economic conditions.

Problematically for business leaders, however, there isn't agreement on what HR transformation actually means or what a successfully "transformed" HR function looks like—the new-fangled organizational structure aside. Ulrich's Element 2 remains elusive. In many companies, HR transformation evolved into a somewhat elaborate tactic to drive down costs and streamline people-related administrative work. In such companies, a "good" HR transformation effort resulted in cost reduction. Problems associated with viewing people issues and resources as simply costs to contain are covered in Chapter 9, "Looking Back and Looking Forward," and it's not necessary to rehash that point here.

Suffice it to say, this lack of definition and objective success metrics are the reasons I consider the HR Transformation movement simply iterative—not ultimately transformational. And I'm not alone.[3]

Even as defined by Ulrich, HR is unmoored from that which drives the business—the creation of value in a company. Even in the most "transformed" HR environment, HR professionals are not tethered to the business strategy or results, nor is their success linked to the success of the organization.

HR transformation produced structural change and opportunities for new systems to link it all together, but lacking a specific connection to purpose (that is, value creation), it ultimately lacks meaningful connection to the business.

Where We Are Now

Without a doubt, HR is on the hot seat. For years, there have been pleas from inside and outside the function to step up the HR game. Business leader reactions have varied from one extreme to another. Some have funded reorganizations, implemented robust and expensive HR technologies, and created elaborate HR outsourcing relationships. Others have threatened to and, in some cases, have eliminated the HR function altogether.[4]

Through all this transformation, the ability of the strategic and analytical HR "partners" and "centers of excellence" to drive business value has yet to materialize. And the patience of many HR customers, sponsors, and stakeholders seems to be waning. From the time *Fast Company* magazine published the article "Why We Hate HR" in 2005, the tone about the function has only gone downhill. HR has been faulted and blamed and further "transformed" in various attempts to make the function more relevant. In 2012, McKinsey teamed up with Corporate Executive Board to publish a

47-page research paper called "The State of Human Capital: False Summit," detailing how far the HR function still has to go. Other studies outline these same problems. Even SHRM—the Society for Human Resource Management—published a teaching guide for the "Why We Hate HR" article, for goodness sake![5]

More recent buzz came out of Ram Charan's article in *Harvard Business Review* blog, "It's Time to Split HR."[6] Charan posits that the strategic part of HR should be split from the more administrative part of HR, which should report to the CFO. This article was countered by Dave Ulrich, writing in the same forum, "Do Not Split HR—At Least Not Ram Charan's Way."[7] His opinion is that splitting the function doesn't solve the strategic issue and only creates a governance dilemma. Ulrich states, "I suggest a holistic approach to helping the middle 60%." Elsewhere in the article, he explains, "I tend not to focus on either 20%. The top 20% are exceptional and don't need help. They should be role models for others. The bottom 20% won't take help. But, the 60% seem, in my view, to be actively engaged in learning how to help their organizations improve."

I disagree with both. Neither, after all, addresses the missing connection between business value creation and critical human capital.

At a time when more money than ever is being spent on human capital technology and consulting, there seems to be scant attention paid to value creation as it relates to hiring, talent development, and employee retention. The financial implications of effective talent management—enhanced quality of hire, greater productivity, reduced attrition—are enormous. It's simple logic to understand that better hires will drive innovation, greater sales, and ultimately market value. But ask your typical HR professional to explain results tied to such metrics, and the response usually includes a wide-eyed stare and murmurings that "systems don't talk," the "data is bad," and "we don't track that."

In our new economy, it is clear that talent rules. Companies with the greater share of smart, high-performing employees win. They are deriving more and more value from the intellectual capabilities of their teams. As illustrated throughout this book, intellectual capital is driving the market values of companies across all industries, and almost exclusively so in some. Look at the intellectual capital value of Facebook, LinkedIn, or Google—nearly their entire market values. Even Walmart, John Deere, and Weyerhaeuser owe more than half their value to IC. "Knowledge workers" are to 2020 what manufacturing assets were to 1970, except this resource is in much shorter supply and is much more portable.

And when it comes to IC value, quality is the only talent metric that matters. Research from Corporate Executive Board underscores the value of a great hire. It's worth repeating here: A "superstar" produces 12 times more than an average performer. And a "star" performer is 3 times more productive. On the flip side, a bad hire actually hurts corporate performance. And let's pile on more data: A Deloitte 2012 study showed that the cost of recruiting, hiring, and training a new professional employee can vary from 2–4 times the position's annual compensation. It doesn't take much imagination to understand how costly turnover—particularly among key knowledge workers—can be for a company.[8]

When you consider that every Googler is in effect expected to grow their fair share of the company's market value, averaging about $5.5 million per employee, it is easy to understand the imperative of talent quality. The higher the IC value of a company, the more relevant the talent quality imperative will be. While talent quality in some roles at GM is imperative, on average, it is not so to the same degree as at Google.

HR itself, however, is still overly entrenched in an industrial context where labor's role was to support the value driver of that age—manufacturing assets. Today, intellectual capital is the value driver, and HR has not been able to adjust to this new context, despite structural transformation.

Even with these structural changes, dramatic advancements in human capital technology, processes, and data, in the absence of a new orientation toward value creation, the dial really has not moved much. Consider these points, based on different PwC and McKinsey 2012 studies:

- Seventy-eight percent of CEOs plan to make changes in their talent strategy.

- Only 31% of CEOs surveyed said they were confident that they have the talent needed to grow their businesses in the near future.

- The majority of CEOs believe human capital information is important but don't receive adequate data.

- And perhaps most shockingly, only 32% of HR leaders have high confidence in their own strategy or actions.

Where else, within the confines of the corporate world, are huge investments made on a daily basis without the ability to quantify value, worth, or results? Companies have calculated the ROI on pruning pennies from mailing lists. Supply chain systems have grown so complex, measurable, and predictive that supplies can be tracked minute by minute as they travel across the world to their destination. Yet every day, employees are hired, talent systems are implemented, performance reviews completed, training boxes checked, and so on— all without the ability to connect their efforts with creating value.

The Real Reasons HR Doesn't Have a Seat at the Table

There are several reasons for the fundamental flaw in the way companies measure the effectiveness of their talent efforts—and much of it lies within the Human Resources function, according to that same McKinsey/Corporate Executive Board 2012 paper.[9]

After considering the research and my own analysis, there are three key reasons that explain why measurable progress related to talent management efforts, outcomes, and predictability have been limited. Behind each of these reasons is a story about how HR has gotten to this place—followed by a discussion of what can be done to turn the ship around.

Lack of HR Credibility

Many corporations have few, if any, strategic positions dedicated to HR. The demands placed on HR aren't financial or analytical in nature because companies don't position the function as such. Overwhelmed with personnel-related administrative responsibilities—and few demands tied to strategy or measurement—individuals in HR roles are viewed as having low "authority." In turn, this causes them to struggle establishing credibility, assessing strategic opportunities, and driving results-based change.

A Support Function Mindset

When jobs are tactical in nature, they appeal to people who like tactical work. Many HR professionals, when surveyed, report a preference for administrative, nonstrategic work. They often have a low tolerance for risk and a limited sense of what they care to "own" or have authority over. Other studies indicate that HR professionals have a lack of confidence in their own skills and abilities, which leads (in general) to choosing administrative work over more strategic, analytical career opportunities. It's not a leap to tie these results and conclusions to the point from an unrelated study, already discussed: Only 32% of HR leaders have high confidence in their own strategy or actions.

Skill and Capability Gaps

Here is where it all comes full-circle. Nonstrategic, administrative jobs attract tactical-minded people who prefer more rote, task-driven work. Couple this with the bona fide difficulty of obtaining accurate, people-related data (that is, measurements related to quality of hire, cost of attrition, ROI of learning investments, and so on) and you've got a lack of data-based decision-making and forecasting that impedes the driving of change. HR leaders are unable to gather and use data to create business cases and, in turn, build a "burning platform" for significant changes or investments in their company's talent strategy.

To further illustrate the reason HR lacks strategic leadership and analytical skills, consider these findings from *The New Talent Management Network's* 2013 "State of Talent Managers Report":

- Most HR incumbents are in the function because they want to help people.
- Only 18% aspire to be CHROs.
- Sixty-eight percent consider themselves to be "top performers," yet...
- Sixty-nine percent stated they have only a "slight" understanding of their company's business.

This survey data indicates that, as mentioned in its conclusions, HR professionals' aspirations are measured, and their preference is more humanistic than capitalistic. Simply put, their love for and interest in people outweighs their love for and interest in the business.

So although structure has been transformed and supportive technologies are being implemented, the evidence points to HR talent itself being the biggest barrier to true transformation. The predominantly administrative skills and attributes that served HR practitioners well in the industrial age are now obsolete. The new skills in defining and leading change, guided by a clear understanding of value creation, are still nearly absent. That is the urgent challenge in looking forward; it is a time bomb for the HR function.

Where We Need to Go

Where HR needs to go seems evident. Spoiler alert: It looks very different from that which we know today.

Many entrepreneurs and start-up CEOs know this already. Their visceral reaction to the notion of hiring a "Human Resources" team is palpable. They equate such employees with an onslaught of bureaucracy and administrivia, while simultaneously understanding that the importance of talent is front and center. In a small startup, the CEO is effectively also the CHRO and spreads the duty out among first hires. From there a range of other models exist—from the larger companies that operate without an HR team by continuing to divvy up work up among managers and leaders or outsource it, to the more famous Netflix example, which claims to have "reinvented HR" by doing away with many traditional HR practices. The resistance, however, is to administrative burden, not to caring for talent.[10]

But at what point in an organization's growth cycle should a "human capital" team be assembled? What is the value in this investment? The development—and evolution—of a measurable talent strategy that reflects deep understanding of and expertise in connecting talent and value creation is the ultimate (and arguably singular) purpose of a new breed of human capital professionals. And herein lies the real difference between the HR function that is needed and the HR function that we have.

What can we learn from how value creation was managed in a past era? In our earlier manufacturing-based economy, Operations required a close connection with Finance to fund and execute economically sound business decisions. Operations understood what could be achieved from a manufacturing standpoint under a variety of investment scenarios. Finance had the expertise to figure the "return" side of the equation to determine which investment scenario made the most economic sense. Operations teams worked with Finance to make these decisions jointly, and together they evaluated the results over time. An entire body of financial tools and expertise grew up to support this relationship, including Cost Accounting, Capital Budgeting, and Activity Based Costing.

The relationship between Operations and Finance developed to that extent because tangible capital was the primary means of value creation and the largest expenditure. Today, human capital is the primary means of value creation and the largest expenditure, yet no equivalent relationship exists between Finance and HR. But it will need to be created. Until that time, organizations cannot maximize people-related financial outcomes and measure the results of these efforts.

Finance and HR: The Odd Couple

Let's face it: You could hardly find two functions in the business world with a more historically contentious relationship. At the root of such discord, after all, is the fact that while "people are our greatest assets," they are also our greatest expense. In general, CFOs see people as impossible to plan, predict, or control—unlike other assets under their purview. CHROs, on the other hand, insist that people require investment, and because they are impossible to plan, predict, or control, measuring the value of that investment is not possible. To make matters worse, CFOs consistently have a "seat at the table" while CHROs are trying to locate the conference room where the meeting is taking place. They are seen as not keeping up, reactionary, and driving "transformation" without purpose or measurable results.

But for an intangible asset-based business to thrive, both of these senior leadership roles must evolve.

It's important to note here that some CFOs may never have the right skills, knowledge, or competencies to work with HR in building a human capital strategy that drives business value. Likewise, some HR leaders might never be the right incumbents to do such work from the people side of the business. This conversation is not about the people currently in those roles, but about the roles themselves. The role of CFO and CHRO, as they exist today, must champion this work and bring it forward in a way unlike that which has been seen before.

Three facts will become the foundation of this new relationship between CFO and CHRO:

1. The impact of intellectual capital on market valuations

2. The demand for human capital—structure, process, organization, leadership, and so on—to increase the value of IC in the future

3. The scarcity of talent to power IC production

The Strategy

The way forward is paved with intellectual capital. As you remember from Chapter 2, "Is Your Most Important Asset Really an Asset?," expected future cash flow is dependent on the performance of intangible assets (intellectual capital) and, by extension, human capital. To realize that expected future cash flow, the company must maximize its relevant intellectual capital. The value-driven talent strategy framework described in Chapters 5, "Identifying Critical Roles Through Work Processes," and 6, "The New Talent Strategy Game Plan," is the way to do so. Bringing that framework to life, the following paragraphs and pages will break down the approach into succinct steps and posit novel roles and responsibilities, as well as discuss historical issues to consider solving along the way.

To develop its talent strategy, a company must first hone its focus on human capital by following these five steps:

1. Gaining understanding among senior leaders about this philosophy and method, and about the need for designing strategy to maximize intellectual capital production.

2. Examining where discernable intellectual capital exists within the organization and determining the relative value of each component.

3. Understanding the talent implications of the most valuable IC components by comparing where the organization currently is to where it needs to be.

4. Committing to the concept of over-investing in talent for critical roles to avoid gaps.

5. Identifying specific organizational goals related to future intellectual capital needs.

After these steps have been taken, it's the open road for those intent on driving the right talent results. Before discussing what follows strategy, though, the question of who drives this effort must be addressed.

Linda: In most companies today, HR reports directly to the CEO. How is it possible then, that so many CEOs claim to be so unhappy with the performance and results of HR? Isn't that ultimately a reflection on them?

Tom: HR is the CEO's landline to the people lever in his business, but the line's been disconnected. I think the CEO's contradictory position is more a result of frustration than anything else. The whole point in paying for any function, in this case HR, is to have the deep expertise required to seize opportunities and solve problems.

The CEO's intuitive sense about people-related business risks is not getting a sufficient response. HR has been left untethered to the economic model by the shift in peoples' roles from labor to knowledge worker. HR isn't positioned to make the best economic decisions in the new model, and they generally lack the skills to recognize and fix this connection. So the CEO knows the expertise is needed but doesn't know how to access it—often, they hire a consulting firm as the last straw!

The Leadership

Who should take charge of such work? The CEO? The CFO? HR? Does this new reality mean that HR professionals need business and finance skills, or does it mean that Finance should learn more about hiring and retaining people? There are no good answers because the questions themselves are rooted in the old framework.

Only a new model can break through the decades of corporate evolution and happenstance, the perception of ineffective roles and functions, and outdated frameworks by which people are managed and costs contained. A new model isn't necessarily about a different organizational structure or a new title. It's about understanding value creation and having the capability to master it. To illustrate this point of view without being distracted by references to traditional titles, I'll refer to this new model as simply the "IC Strategy Team." This team ensures the development and particularly the execution of a value-driven talent strategy.

Consider this new IC Strategy Team as being a hybrid of traditional HR and Finance professionals, with deep expertise in three fundamental areas:

1. The way in which assets are allocated to power the business
2. The attraction, selection, and retention of a high-performing, diverse workforce
3. Analytics and measurement

Given this construct, existing roles such as CHRO, the CFO, COO—even the CEO—would be reshaped as the IC lever is pulled and as other levers, less critical to business value, take a backseat.

The Process

As with any sound effort to power a strategy, the work begins with defining the processes that will enable it. From this process design comes clarity about activities, technology, people, and measures.

As the process is built, we must keep the guiding principles of this effort in mind—most importantly, *increasing business value, over-investing in critical roles* and *measuring efforts and results*. These guiding principles act as guardrails during process design discussions and ultimately help shape the way in which we get to the goal.

Processes need to be defined for each of the following:

• Regular assessment of the organizational implications of business growth strategies, connected with the IC value that will be produced, including an evaluation of current versus future talent needs.

• Determining the right talent decisions—build/buy/borrow—to fulfill critical needs on a regular basis.

- Differentiated methods of continuously ensuring talent for critical roles:

    - **Talent acquisition**—Sourcing, attracting, selecting and onboarding

    - **Talent management**—Development, assessment, rewards and retention

    - **Talent hedging**—Sourcing and contracting for limited term critical resources

- Assessing talent quality for critical roles to identify the investments that have resulted in hiring and retaining the highest performing people. See Chapter 7, "The Only Metric that Matters," for more information about the recommended approach to managing this process.

The difference between talent processes led by an "IC Strategy Team," intent on over-investing in critical roles, as compared to the typical HR approach, cannot be overstated. Consider the following, which uses talent acquisition as an example.

The typical approach to talent acquisition:

- Open position requisitions prioritized by time—like milk—with a first-in, first-out method of queuing.

- All requisitions managed in essentially the same way with recruiters taking their lead from the more demanding or opinionated hiring managers regarding how a job should be filled.

- Sourcing methods limited largely to posting jobs on job boards or LinkedIn, with very little time or effort dedicated to finding and wooing passive candidates.

- An understaffed team of lowly-paid, junior recruiters working 40 or more requisitions at once, often dealing with varied job functions and types, a multitude of hiring managers, and little if any process rigor. In such an environment, the role they play defaults to administrative.

- Hiring managers with little understanding of how the process should work, how candidates should be managed, and how to select great talent.

The "IC Strategy Team" approach to talent acquisition:

- A talent acquisition team built to differentiate between critical and noncritical roles in terms of invested resources per hire, while delivering acceptable results in line with pre-determined metrics for each category of hiring:

  - Critical roles assigned to a team of highly skilled and compensated researchers and recruiters who work closely with hiring managers to find, pipeline, screen, and close the most qualified candidates. A robust and proactive method of finding and marketing to candidates for these roles is modeled after the Investor Relations approach (see Chapter 8, "Attracting and Retaining the Human Capitalist Investor"). When required, this team has the capability to rival search firms in surgically finding and removing talent from other occupations or companies.

  - Harder-to-fill, noncritical roles are supported by a team of highly skilled recruiters, leveraging tools and technology to research, target, and sell passive candidates.

  - Noncritical positions considered easy to fill are supported by junior recruiters before passing the most qualified candidates on to hiring managers.

Examples of Traditional HR Processes that Need to Change

There are a host of commonplace HR processes and practices that, when considered in the IC light, make little if any sense the way they are currently conducted. Consider the following:

- **New hire orientation**

  In most organizations, formal orientation programs are unvaried and required for all. In fact, employee start dates are often dictated by the scheduling of these programs. Typically led by junior HR or administrative team members, they usually focus on completing paperwork and lectures on matters considered essential for compliance. Arguably a bad experience for anyone, this can be a disastrous first introduction for key talent the company has just invested untold dollars and time in enticing them to join.

- **Management "101" training for all managers**

  In general, these types of programs completely disregard the amount or type of training new leaders have had before joining their current company—not a minor detail given the frequency of job changes professionals typically make by the mid-point of their career. These programs are also perceived as notoriously ineffective and typically lack measures tied to behavioral changes or objective outcomes. Most importantly in the context of IC, however, training for managers who are responsible for leading a team of service workers—for example, technicians, retail employees, call center staff, and so on—should look much different than training for those leading teams of knowledge workers—software developers, engineers, researchers. Most leadership development teams would be hard-pressed to explain how such training would differ for this latter group, much less how to implement and evaluate it.

- **Succession planning**

  Succession planning takes place in many organizations and provides an important rigor around talent calibration and planning. But often, the process takes place by level without regard to where the most critical roles lie within the organization. So while succession reviews may go wide (say, for all VPs), they don't go deep (for a key area of the business like, for example, research), where the most critical roles—and the need to identify successors—lie.

- **Employee engagement surveys**

  For this example, let's go back to our Beatles analogy. Imagine if an HR manager had conducted a typical engagement survey for the Beatles organization, including the Fab Four themselves as well as their entire team—roadies, the marketing and promotions team, merchandise, catering, management, even the guitar tuners. One person equals one vote, as is the case with engagement surveys. Paul McCartney's feedback would have equal weight to that of the guitar tuner's. What then would happen if the results showed that the majority of the team was unhappy with the communication or the development planning processes—while the Fab Four was in fact pleased with how those things were? And on the other hand, what if the Fab Four felt that rewards and recognition were really, really bad, while the majority of employees indicated these things were great? The typical employee engagement process is flawed in that it is a game of averages. What is paramount, arguably, is how a company's most critical talent (regardless of function, department, or level) feels—and what they believe they need in order to be successful.

I could go on: compensation policies and methods that limit the earnings of the most valuable employees, exit interviews that target the masses instead of pinpointing the most critical talent, and so on.

The point is clear—the typical approach of HR is one of parity and equity; all programs and processes implemented and managed with (essentially) sameness for all employees. This attempt to make things "fair" for employees and mitigate risk is often at the expense of business results and, as such, in fact creates longer-term risk for everyone.

Over-Investing in Critical Roles: The Impact on Everyone Else

This "over-investing" may or may not be evident to others in the organization, so defending it in that way is not the point. The point is that it's an essential strategy for sustaining the creation of business value. Employees have enough maturity and business sense to understand the reasons for over-investing in key talent, or they can get there easily enough with the right information. Take Apple, for example, where employees working in Accounts Payable or Legal certainly understand the importance of the Product Designers and Software Engineers to the success of the overall business. In fact, their own success depends on the success of those in these critical roles. They know that to be true, and it would be disingenuous to pretend they don't. Finally, if asked, they would probably applaud the logic—and business value—in an approach that over-invests in those key roles. After all, a rising tide lifts all boats.

Finally, narrowly targeting the best talent approaches to a defined group of critical employees allows a leadership team to identify those practices that have merit being invested in and rolled out (most likely in a streamlined, efficient way) more broadly across the organization. This enables a company to define their own path and chart it forward, beginning with the most critical parts of the business and moving outward.

Linda: The magnitude of change this implies for HR is huge, on top of the constant shifting that most HR teams have already been through. If I were an HR leader who embraced these concepts, where would I begin?

Tom: In my view you would start by defining where you wanted to end up. What is your destination? No matter what that destination entails, it must include understanding critical roles. In addition, the people in those roles need to be treated as assets. Many other attributes of the destination should be clearly articulated, including the role of managers.

The reason for having a destination is to be able to plan and track steps toward that point and to determine along the way which actions are on the strategic path and which are not. The specific steps to take, how big they are, and how soon to take them depends entirely on the circumstances, but the discipline of identifying a destination is the best starting point.

The Outcomes

In such a construct, the necessary outcomes become crystal clear. Simply put, an organization needs to answer these questions:

- Do we know, objectively, which are the most critical roles?
- Are we able to differentiate performance in these roles?
- Are we are hiring top-performing employees into our most critical roles?
- How well are we engaging and retaining critical talent?
- How successfully are we producing the intellectual capital that drives our market value?

The processes that enable the overall value-driven talent strategy will indicate discrete data points at which process performance can be measured; here are a few that would be considered essential:

- **Talent Acquisition**
  - Where did our highest quality, most critical talent come from, and what actions are we taking to get more from these sources?
  - How complete is the pipeline for mission critical positions, and what actions are we taking to keep candidates engaged, interested, and informed?
  - What do the candidates—at all stages of the process—perceive of the experience, and how can we continue to improve?

- **Talent Management**
  - How well do we solicit, listen to, and respond to input from critical talent regarding talent processes, engagement strategies, and execution of both?
  - How effective are leaders of knowledge workers? How do we measure and how can we continually improve results of this pivotal responsibility?
  - Why do we lose critical talent? How useful are our turnover analytics at identifying reasons and solving for regrettable losses?

In the end, the "IC Strategy Team" approach doesn't represent a tweaking of the current Finance or HR model; it calls for a complete overhaul of what defines success and how we get there in our knowledge-driven economy. Finance understands and can model business value with more aptitude than HR. In the absence of action, sooner or later external forces will knock over the first domino that sets this work in motion—as explained in Chapter 9. Knowing that knowledge workers in critical roles ultimately drive that business value, HR has a leg up on defining methods that can supply and retain those workers. A melding of these capabilities is needed to generate the right business solution, to develop and execute a value-driven talent strategy.

What is yet to be seen: Who takes charge and runs with this opportunity? Will it be HR in the driver's seat, truly acting as a business leader and seizing the chance to add real, measurable business value despite the extent of the change it will demand? Or will HR be taken along for the ride, pushed and prodded by the CEO or Finance until they are forced into changing or dying out?

It's time for HR to chart its own path. HR must forge ahead with innovation to produce real business value or come to terms with being the next Walkman—overtaken by faster and better competition.

Endnotes

1. http://www.macworld.com/article/1163179/how_the_ipod_changed_the_world_of_music.html.

2. Dave Ulrich arguably caused a firestorm in 1997 with his book, *Human Resource Champions*. Amy Kates, Downey Kates Associates, puts it best in *(Re)Designing the HR Organization* (Human Resource Planning Society Journal 29.2), where she notes: "Over the last decade there has been a profound shift in the work of the HR function. The publication in 1997 of Dave Ulrich's Human Resource Champions spurred HR leaders across various industries to realign their organizations to undertake "strategic business partner" work. At the same time, a focus on cost cutting and efficiency aimed at staff functions in general—and at HR in particular—has pushed much HR transaction work into shared services or to outsourced vendors. For many HR departments, this process of "transformation," as it is popularly called, has been a wrenching experience.

3. http://www.pwc.com/us/en/people-management/publications/assets/pwc-hfs-hr-transform.pdf and http://www.deloitte.com/assets/Dcom-China/Local%20Assets/Documents/HRT_White_Paper(1).pdf.

4. http://online.wsj.com/articles/SB10001424052702304819004579489603299910562 and http://www.nytimes.com/2012/12/02/jobs/more-companies-are-outsourcing-their-human-resources-work.html.

5. https://www.shrm.org/Education/hreducation/Documents/Why_We_Hate_HR_Teaching_Guide_FINAL_4-06.pdf.

6. https://hbr.org/2014/07/its-time-to-split-hr.

7. https://hbr.org/2014/07/do-not-split-hr-at-least-not-ram-charans-way.

8. PwC, "Key Trends in Human Capital 2012: A Global Perspective," PwC Saratoga's 2012/2013 "US Human Capital Effectiveness Report."

9. http://www.google.com/url?sa=t&rct=j&q=&esrc=s&source=web&cd=1&ved=0CB8QFjAA&url=http%3A%2F%2Fwww.mckinsey.com%2F~%2Fmedia%2Fmckinsey%2Fdotcom%2Fclient_service%2Forganization%2Fpdfs%2Fstate_of_human_capital_2012.ashx&ei=WmN2VND0IIymNvH4gtAO&usg=AFQjCNGFt7i_cDJqiKeF-0BrzvZ89Ma6qg&bvm=bv.80642063,d.eXY.

10. http://online.wsj.com/news/articles/SB10001424052702304819004579489603299910562 and https://hbr.org/2014/01/how-netflix-reinvented-hr.

Conclusion

Should we immediately stop functioning as we have in the past, trade in outmoded tools and practices, and focus talent strategy exclusively on intellectual capital? Probably not—the shift required will not likely happen overnight.

A visit to the local hardware store is proof enough that one economic age doesn't simply end while another begins. There are still plenty of shovels, axes, saws, hammers, and pretty much any other hand tool that was standard fare in the preindustrial, artisanal world. By the same token, the trappings of the industrial world aren't going away anytime soon either.

The industrial age, fueled by science and new sources of energy in the mid-eighteenth century, has seen vastly more productivity than any other time in the history of the world. From what we know, the pace of productivity will be eclipsed in the age we're now in, the *information age*. An economic hallmark of this post-industrial period is the predominance and capacity of knowledge in creating value. As demonstrated throughout this book, value produced by knowledge workers is pervasive, having a positive impact on most every industry.

Another historical fact is that tools and methods needed for managing productivity can barely be imagined, much less created, when the means of production change so dramatically and so rapidly. For example, it took over 100 years for the managerial and financial accounting standards that we now take for granted to be established and documented. Both of these accounting areas eventually became professions in and of themselves and are now essential to successfully managing complex industrial businesses and providing reliable information to investors. There is no doubt that these practices contributed to more profitable businesses and more effective investments.

Although it is more the case that the information age "began" than it is the industrial age "ended," how various businesses have adapted to this evolution and the consequences of their decisions have led to very different realities. U.S. Leather, American Beet Sugar, and Bethlehem Steel all once reigned in the Dow Jones Industrial Average, but as the industrial age waned, they faded into the background or entirely disappeared from the planet.

Other players with roots in the same era as those just mentioned have fared differently. Three companies profiled earlier in the book are good examples of this:

- Conagra Foods was formed in 1919 through consolidation of four grain mills in Nebraska. As discussed in Chapter 3, "Valuing and Evaluating Companies and Their Intellectual Capital," Conagra evolved from this pure commodity business into a consumer products giant over the decades that followed. Today, Conagra has an enterprise value that is 88% intellectual capital, owing to a large portfolio of well-developed brands.

- 3M Company began as Minnesota Mining and Manufacturing, mining rocks on the shores of Lake Superior in 1902 as raw material for a sandpaper business. Although initially a mining enterprise, 3M has had an innovative mind-set throughout most of its history. As profiled in Chapter 5, "Identifying Critical Roles Through Work Processes," the company now spends nearly $2 billion annually on research that drives its market valuation and 84% IC share of enterprise value.

- UPS opened shop as a messenger service in Seattle in 1907. As described earlier in the book, UPS is today, in effect, a technology firm that delivers packages. This fact is reflected in a market valuation that far exceeds its industry average and results in intellectual capital being 91% of enterprise value (refer to Chapter 3). This is in contrast to the struggling U.S. Postal Service, its erstwhile competitor (to Ben Franklin's dismay!).

These three companies were somehow able to take advantage of the opportunity to create value and sustain their enterprises through knowledge. They successfully flipped from being valued for their tangible assets to being valued for intangible assets—while others flopped.

What is the next hurdle to be passed as companies evolve in the information age? It is to take control and manage this new means of production rather than relying on serendipitous circumstances for their value creation.

It might be easier for companies in brand new industries like biotechnology and information technology to make this leap because the need and value are so apparent to them. At the same time, those entities are often inclined to throw out inferior HR tools of the past without necessarily having proven replacements available for them. Whether they can scale effectively enough in a competitive environment without all the tools needed at their disposal remains to be seen.

Old school industries sometimes seem to grab at whatever appears to be a value-creating resource in the intellectual capital space, often with mixed results. Almost regardless of where you look, every industry has latched onto the allure of "brand building," impulsively tapping marketing talent from the likes of P&G and hoping for similar results. But what works well for a consumer products company like P&G doesn't necessarily translate with the same value to the financial services or healthcare industries. In the absence of proven strategies, the types of intellectual capital that can most effectively be layered onto traditional businesses, and the types of human capital required, are questions that must also pass the test of time.

Current efforts may be fine when it comes to low hanging fruit, but a more considered approach will be required to drive sustainable growth via intellectual capital in the future.

One of the most important questions to ask is where to start. A good starting point would simply be recognizing the components of market value in your business outside of traditional financial statements. By viewing true enterprise value from a balance sheet standpoint, what is revealed are the areas of opportunity to proactively invest in critical roles, which produce intellectual capital and drive cash flow (see Figure C.1). This reveals the critical roles where talent must be viewed for what it is, an asset rather than a cost. This starting point provides a gateway for beginning to construct human capital plans in line with the value-driven talent strategy model described in Chapter 5.

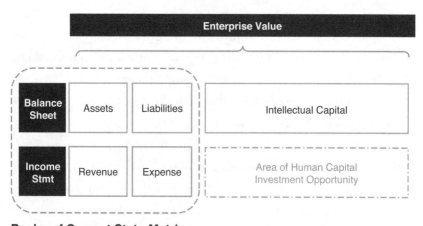

Figure C.1 Gateway—Areas of Opportunity.
© 2014 Human Capital Formation, LLC

We discussed the future of financial reporting regarding intellectual and human capital in Chapter 9, "Looking Back and Looking Forward," which is inevitable. More often than not, when an issue comes down to compliance, work is started as late as possible, and the target is set to meet minimum standards. This is not one of those issues; it would behoove organizations to recognize this and capitalize on it by taking action now.

The future compliance requirements, whatever form they eventually take, reflect a pervading gap in information and capability necessary to effectively operate a knowledge-driven business. This need also implies a function within companies that has never existed before and lies somewhere between what Human Resources and Finance are today (refer to Chapters 9 and 10, "Who Is Responsible? What Is the Purpose of HR?"). These two functions are the best equipped to define the future and create the appropriate path, but they must do so together; each have blind spots that would impair going at it alone. Time not spent taking steps in the direction of tackling this issue is time that creates risk rather than value.

One of the reasons it will be difficult for companies to decide what action to take is the divergence of circumstances across industries and organizations and the practicality of investing in the future versus dealing with the tyranny of the urgent. Although all companies can benefit from utilizing the value-driven talent strategy approach, a sensible self-assessment of where a company falls on the scale of relevance to this work is worthwhile. Companies should consider where they aspire to be in the future—rather than where they find themselves now (see Figure C.2). The farther a company falls to the right on this assessment tool, the more relevant and urgent this work is. These factors of market value, workforce, and talent focus generally fall along industry lines, although UPS, as previously discussed, is a good example where that is not the case.

It is entirely possible that a company could fall on the intangible side of market value (right side) and the labor side of workforce. This would be the case for UPS and for Proctor & Gamble, for example. The talent focus for both of those may fall right in the middle. Google, on the other hand, is likely all on the right-hand side. Whatever the case may be, it is informative as to what strategies should be considered and with what urgency.

Figure C.2 Self-Assessing for Relevance.

© 2014 Human Capital Formation, LLC

And finally, what can we conclude about the value of talent?

We know the value of human capital is the discounted present value of the additional productivity of people above and beyond that of unskilled labor derived from their knowledge and abilities.

We know that companies are valued by calculating the discounted present value of future expected cash flows. We also know that growth in market values today is primarily due to increases in intellectual capital that in turn drive cash flow. The unique source of this intellectual capital is talent—and the human capital they possess.

Theoretically, if you could isolate one person and the intellectual capital he or she produces and associate that directly with the cash flow it drives, you could calculate the value of that person's human capital contribution (and factoring in that person's cost, even the return on investment!). Unfortunately, that is not the way things work in practice. Teams of knowledge workers produce intellectual capital, and managers apply additional knowledge along the way. Various types of intellectual capital come together to drive specific cash flow (patents and customer relationships for example). Cash flow in this sense is a multivariate function of knowledge workers that can't practically be isolated to the level of an individual.

What *can* be said is productivity of knowledge workers varies, and the more productive each is, the more value can be produced. Productivity can be measured, at least on a relative basis, and we have called that measure "quality" in this book (see Chapter 7, "The Only Metric that Matters"). Therefore, any investment that increases the overall quality of talent, and is less costly than the cash flow it produces, will have a positive return. Given what we know about the value of human capital productivity, the bar for investments is a low one. Said another way, the impact of efforts that successfully increase the quality of talent in critical roles[1] is almost certainly worth the cost.

A fair analogy of the relationship between knowledge workers and cash flow can be found when considering a symphony orchestra. Think about all the positions involved: the musicians themselves, the sound manager, the stagehands, and so on. No matter what anyone else does, a symphony orchestra that employs the most prodigious cellist in the world but is accompanied by a host of mediocre musicians will not impress an audience. The product of their effort is collective. Calculating the value of any one musician will be limited by the worth of their collective output. The metric that matters most is obvious; we have one prodigy and 100 or so average musicians...quality is imperative across the board in these highest value-producing roles, and quality is the only logical proxy for value.

Roles other than musicians add to the success of the orchestra, including those who set up the stage, fulfill ticket orders, schedule events, and process the payroll. These roles are all important, but quality of the magnitude required from the musicians is unnecessary. If it were, I imagine it would be hard to make ends meet. In fact many of those roles will be contracted or outsourced at competitive prices rather than directly employed by the orchestra organization.

Humanism Dominates; Capitalism Differentiates

> Our interest in helping others to learn and grow attracts us to the HR profession. In fact, 77% of us consider it to be a primary reason for being in this field. The next most popular reason—helping a company to maximize its profitability—is a distant second at 58%. Those with "Humanistic" reasons for being in HR far outnumber those with "Capitalistic" reasons. However, those with more Capitalistic reasons report faster career growth and are more willing to sacrifice to succeed.
>
> —(New Talent Managers Network, *State of Talent Managers Report*, 2013).

Thank goodness for those apparently willing to sacrifice and have faster career growth in HR! There is a time and place for everything. Milton Freedman observed the following: "Skill as a hunter and trapper had a high value in eighteenth- and nineteenth-century America, a much lower value in twentieth-century America."[2] HR's origination as Labor Relations absolutely required a humanistic predisposition. Child labor, safety, unfair wages—the long list of wrongs associated with industrial employment persist today in many venues, foreign and domestic. Humanistic predisposition is without question important to everyone's character regardless of the age in which we live. But just as striving for fair labor treatment has been necessary for sustaining an industrial economy, recognizing and managing human capital as assets is necessary in building a knowledge economy—and it requires different skills and inclinations. In both cases, the objective is to advance value creation, adhere to sound principles, and maximize benefits for every stakeholder.

We sincerely hope this book stokes imaginations, offers practical thoughts, and contributes to the body of work that advances the productivity of human capital, the talent that owns it, and the enterprises that stimulate it.

Endnotes

1. As we have defined both "quality" and "critical roles" in this book.

2. *Free to Choose*, Milton & Rose Friedman, Harcourt Brace Jovanovich, 1980.

Appendix

American Federation of Labor and Congress of Industrial Organizations

October 5, 2001

Timothy S. Lucas
Director of Research and Technical Activities
Financial Accounting Standards Board
401 Merritt 7
Norwalk, CT 06856-5116

Letter of Comment No: 48
File Reference: 1123-001
Date Received: 10|5|01

Dear Mr. Lucas:

This comment is submitted on behalf of the American Federation of Labor and Congress of Industrial Organizations ("AFL-CIO") in response to the Financial Accounting Standards Board's ("FASB's") request for comments on a potential new agenda project on "Disclosure of Information About Intangible Assets not Recognized in Financial Statements." Collectively bargained pension funds providing retirement security to AFL-CIO union members hold over $3.5 trillion in assets, including over $400 billion in funds directly sponsored by AFL-CIO affiliate unions.

We wholeheartedly support the idea of a new FASB project on disclosure regarding intangible assets. Worker funds approach the question of intellectual capital reporting as long-term investors seeking to obtain the best returns to provide for beneficiaries' retirement security. But they also have the distinct perspective of worker-shareholders, a perspective that is particularly attuned to the importance of workers' knowledge, skills and commitment to the creation of value for shareholders. Although this comment letter focuses on human capital disclosure, we do not mean to imply that FASB's work should be addressed only to that issue.

As discussed in FASB's request for comment and the reports cited therein, the world's leading economies are increasingly knowledge-based. Yet financial reporting has not changed to reflect those new economic realities. While value is more and more created by the skills of a company's workforce, financial reporting is still overwhelmingly focused on tangible assets.

Shareholders recognize the importance of intangible assets to a company's success. This awareness is evident from the fact that the stocks of successful companies trade at significant multiples of book value. Shareholders, then, see a firm's brands, the loyalty of its customers and the human capital of its workforce as critical.

Page 2

Shareholders have also shown an interest in receiving more information on these intangibles. Shareholder proposals seeking disclosure of information on diversity and equal employment opportunity are supported by substantial numbers of shareholders. And a significant number of shareholders have also backed proposals to require executive pay to be linked to employee-related measures, which would lead to a more in-depth discussion of those measures in the company proxy statement. Indeed, UAL Corporation, the parent of United Air Lines, recently implemented a shareholder proposal asking for human-capital-related measures such as employee satisfaction, training and participation to be used in setting executive pay.

Currently, investments in intangibles such as human capital, which produce revenue over a number of years, are treated as current expenses. That treatment violates the basic accounting principle of matching expenses and revenues. We believe that it is appropriate to capitalize expenditures that create value, and we view the work of Lev and Zarowin as suggesting avenues of appropriate inquiry for FASB. We believe that in the context of the ongoing effort to harmonize global accounting standards, FASB should be sensitive to differing approaches among major economies to disclosure in this area, particularly in regard to workforce training and development expenses. However, because there is strong empirical evidence on the returns to such investments, some form of reporting of such expenses should be required.

In addition, we believe that additional disclosure regarding intangibles will bring a much-needed long-term focus to the process for setting executive compensation. Currently, executive incentive compensation usually defines performance by reference to stock price or certain selected accounting measures, none of which may accurately capture a company's investment in intellectual capital. Requiring companies to quantify their human capital investments as a distinct financial reporting item and to provide additional information that allows comparisons between companies will encourage boards of directors to use measures of intellectual capital preservation and development in setting executive pay.

In sum, the increasing importance of human capital and other intangibles is a trend that is not likely to be reversed. As long as financial reporting remains primarily focused on tangible investments, there will be an ever-widening gap between what is shown on a company's balance sheet and both its historic expenditures and its current real value-creating assets.

We would be pleased to be of further assistance to FASB as it explores these issues. I can be reached at (202) 637-3900. Thank you for your consideration.

Very truly yours,

Bill Patterson
Director, Office of Investment

Letter of Comment No: 44
File Reference: 1123-001
Date Received: 9|28|01

American Accounting Association Financial Accounting Standards Committee

**Response to the FASB Invitation to Comment on the Proposal for a New Agenda Project -
"Disclosure of Information About Intangible Assets Not Recognized in Financial Statements"**

Laureen A. Maines, Chair; Eli Bartov, Patricia Fairfield,
D. Eric Hirst, Teresa A. Iannaconi, Russell Mallett,
Catherine M. Schrand, Douglas J. Skinner, Linda Vincent

September 28, 2001

Preamble

The Financial Accounting Standards Committee of the American Accounting Association (hereafter, the Committee) is charged with responding to requests for input from standard-setters on financial reporting issues. The Committee is pleased to respond to the FASB's invitation to comment on the Proposal for a New Agenda Project – Disclosure of Information About Intangible Assets Not Recognized in Financial Statements (hereafter – the Proposal). The opinions in this letter reflect the views of the individuals on the Committee and not those of the American Accounting Association.

Scope of this letter

This letter speaks to the issues raised in the Proposal specifically. In particular, we note that this letter is a precursor to a more-comprehensive letter on intangibles by the Committee that will summarize and evaluate the relatively large literature on this topic and that will focus on issues related to recognition and measurement, as well as disclosure. We expect to submit this letter to the Board before our annual meeting with the Board next May.

General comments

The Committee is broadly supportive of the FASB's proposal for considering issues related to the disclosure and recognition of intangibles. In particular, we agree with the general notion that there are currently inconsistencies in the accounting treatment of economically similar intangibles; for example, the difference between the treatment of intangibles acquired externally and those developed internally. However, we have some reservations and other comments about the Proposal as it currently stands, which fall into the following areas:

1. Disclosure approach.
2. FASB agenda criteria.
3. Pertinent research evidence.

1. Disclosure approach

The Committee has some concerns about the general premise of the Proposal to mandate the footnote disclosures of certain information regarding intangibles. These concerns may be summarized as follows.

In our view, the current Proposal does not provide a convincing case that the proposed disclosures have net benefits to capital market participants or other users of financial statements. Instead, the Proposal simply asserts a popular (in the financial press and among certain commentators) argument that: (1) the current financial reporting and disclosure regime for intangibles is somehow deficient, and (2) the proposed mandated disclosures will correct this deficiency.[1] In our view, these arguments are neither clearly laid out nor supported by convincing evidence.

We have little evidence that speaks to the benefits and costs of disclosures on intangibles. If the FASB is to step in and (say) mandate the disclosure of certain information on intangibles, a question that seems relevant is: why have firms chosen not to disclose this information voluntarily?[2] One answer is that there are likely to be costs associated with such disclosures, including both costs associated with measuring intangibles and proprietary costs of disclosing such information to competitors. Another answer may be that the benefits of these disclosures are not very large, perhaps because these disclosures are not very informative to investors due to low relevance or imprecise measurement. Whatever the case, it seems to us that the relatively low levels of voluntary disclosure in the intangibles area raise the possibility that disclosures in this area do not provide net benefits. In other words, we are concerned that the document seems to proceed on the assumption that the current "approach is suboptimal" (p. 2). Our preliminary contention is that we know little, in terms of evidence, about whether the current disclosure environment for intangibles is "suboptimal" and how mandated disclosures would correct this apparent market failure.[3] We would therefore encourage the FASB to investigate the costs and benefits of intangibles disclosures further, rather than assuming that mandated disclosures in this area provide net benefits.

The Proposal advocates a "disclosure" approach but indicates that this could be a first step towards the recognition of intangible assets in financial statements. We have concerns about how this process – moving from a disclosure regime to a recognition regime – is expected to work. One rationale for such an approach is that by allowing preparers to experiment, through disclosure, with the measurement of certain intangibles, preparers will have time to resolve measurement issues. However, this suggests that initial footnote disclosures on intangibles will have considerable measurement error, which may lead users to view intangible disclosures as relatively uninformative. Additionally, disclosure of information on intangibles may lead users to interpret this information differently precisely because it is footnote information and so indicated to be less reliable (e.g., Bernard and Schipper 1994). Perhaps the Board can consider its own experience in the area of accounting for derivative securities where the Board also started out with a disclosure approach (in SFAS-105, SFAS-107, and SFAS-119) before ultimately arriving at a final statement dealing with recognition (SFAS-133). Looking back, what were the advantages and disadvantages of this approach, and in particular, did the experience gained with the early disclosure statements help resolve the subsequent recognition issues? Is there any part of this experience that can be used to help inform the Board on how best to proceed in the area of intangibles?

If information is to be disclosed, perhaps it should be limited to information that can be reliably measured and verified by auditors. At page 5, the Proposal lists four possible types of disclosures, which we briefly comment on in turn.

- Major classes of intangible assets and their characteristics. How would "major" classes be defined? Would this be a firm or industry level determination (here we could envision issues arising analogous

---

[1] For example, on p. 1 the Proposal asserts that one of the principal goals of the project would be to "improve the quality of information currently being provided—information vital to well-reasoned investment and credit resource allocation decisions." We are not aware of specific arguments or evidence that suggests that current resource allocation decisions in the economy are suboptimal or of evidence on how the proposed disclosures would "fix" this problem.

[2] This is documented in the recent Steering Committee Report of the Business Reporting Research Project, "Improving Business Reporting: Insights into Enhancing Voluntary Disclosures" (FASB, 2001).

[3] For a general discussion of market failures in the context of accounting information, see Leftwich (1980).

to those in the segment reporting area – firms might choose to define disclosure classes so broadly that the disclosures might become meaningless)? On the other hand, if flexibility is not permitted (the FASB defines these classes), how will the rules reflect the diversity that we observe across firms and industries in terms of the nature of the intangibles that are important? That is, we question whether a "one size fits all" disclosure policy is feasible in the area of intangibles given substantial diversity in the economic nature of intangible assets across firms and industries. Moreover, the Conceptual Framework provides limited guidance to resolve these disclosure issues, a point we return to below.

- Expenditures to develop and maintain intangibles. Since expenditures can be measured reliably and verified, it seems that providing more detailed disaggregation than currently available in the financial statements may be informative to investors. However, deciding how to disaggregate expenditures is problematic if there are difficulties in deciding on, say, how the major classes of intangibles would be determined. Additionally, requiring such disaggregation raises issues of consistency in the sense that perhaps finer disclosures in other areas of financial reporting should be required as well.

- Values of intangible assets. We have little evidence on how precisely the values of intangibles assets can be measured, especially since the nature of many intangibles is such that they are difficult to value on a stand-alone basis. As Lev (2001, Ch. 2) indicates, intangibles are characterized by a lack of well-defined property rights, "spillover" effects, etc., which leads in turn to a lack of well-established secondary markets for intangibles. These factors suggest that the measurement issues related to the valuation of intangibles will be substantial. Again, we are reminded of recent experiences in the area of financial instruments where non-trivial measurement issues arise with certain financial assets (and liabilities) that have fairly well-defined, agreed upon, and contractable cash flows. We suspect that valuation issues related to intangibles will be substantially more difficult to resolve than those already encountered in the area of financial instruments, and so are dubious about the reliability of information pertaining to the value of intangibles.

- Significant events that change the anticipated future benefits arising from intangible assets. How precisely would "significant" be defined here? Would it be defined in general across all intangible assets, or for individual classes of intangibles? If "significant" means that an event has occurred that has caused a material (in the legal sense) change in the value of an asset, is this provision not redundant with the SEC disclosure rules and securities laws?

2. FASB Agenda Criteria

Regarding whether this project satisfies the four FASB agenda criteria (p. 6), we question whether criterion (c) – technical feasibility – is satisfied. As the document indicates, the Conceptual Framework provides only general guidance about disclosure issues, and so it is unclear how the Board will resolve issues related to the disclosure of intangibles information without some type of framework. In particular, we can envision that, in developing a standard on the disclosure of information about intangibles, the FASB will have to decide among: (a) alternative pieces of information to disclose, and (b) alternative ways of disclosing that information. Without a stated framework for making such choices, it is unclear how the Board will proceed – what decision criteria will be used? If these types of decisions cannot be made, it would seem more likely that the resulting disclosure statement will leave these issues up to preparers to decide, which will give them the ability, if they so choose, to make fairly vague and uninformative disclosures.

We also believe there may be an issue related to criterion (d) – practical consequences. In particular, one piece of "evidence" cited by proponents of the need to provide more information regarding intangibles was the large and increasing difference between many firms' market capitalization and book values, a trend that became especially apparent during the 1990s. For example, it was not uncommon for firms in the high-technology sector to have market-to-book ratios in the double-digits during the internet "boom" years of 1998 and 1999. Some interpreted these ratios as evidence of the importance of a new business model in which intangible assets such as intellectual capital had become a key "value driver" for these firms. The fact that stock prices, especially those in the high tech sector, have declined fairly steadily since the early part of last year may reduce the persuasive power of these types of arguments, lessening the risk of any potential intervention by either the SEC or Congress. Moreover, the relatively high levels of stock market volatility evident over the last 2-3 years also speaks to concerns about the wisdom of using stock market prices as a benchmark for assessing the relevance of reported book values.

3. Pertinent Research Evidence

We are concerned that the proponents of the document are accepting popular arguments at face value, without consideration of the evidence. For example, consider the statement (p. 6) that "financial reports continue to fail to provide information about what many argue are increasingly the main drivers of values in the capital markets." We are not aware of any specific arguments or evidence that supports statements such as this.

In addition, the proposal indicates that "(t)he substantial body of research by Professor Baruch Lev of New York University and others...should be of considerable interest in resolving the principal issues in this project (p. 4)." As indicated above, we plan to provide a fuller review of academic research in the intangibles area in a subsequent letter, but think it is relevant to indicate two points regarding intangibles research here. First, the Proposal takes the position that the supposed deficiencies in the area of financial reporting for intangibles can be "fixed" by providing additional footnote disclosures. However, the research referred to, by Professor Lev and others, does not directly speak to the issue of the benefits and costs of disclosure. Second, much of the research in this area uses the "value relevance" methodology. As Holthausen and Watts (2001) have recently discussed, these studies have recognized limitations, especially in terms of their applicability to standard-setting. For example, these studies tend to assume that equity market participants are the preeminent users of financial statement information, and sometimes ignore the need for financial information to be reliable and hence verifiable. Moreover, these studies have recognized methodological limitations that become more pronounced when applied to assets, such as intangibles, that are difficult to trade and which earn economic "rents."

Several academic studies address the general topic of whether financial statement information has become more or less "relevant" through time (measured as the extent of the association between stock prices and financial statement information).[4] Although the findings in this area are not completely consistent, it would be hard to reach a conclusion from this research that the relevance of financial statement information in general has declined through time.

Conclusion

To summarize our position, the Committee supports the spirit of the Board's proposal to initiate a project related to the disclosure and possible recognition of intangibles. Our concerns arise in the area of how best to go about this process. As we indicate in this letter, it seems to us that there are some difficult issues that the Board will have to address in implementing even the apparently simple task of increasing the amount of information disclosed about intangibles.

---

[4] Three representative studies are Collins, Maydew, and Weiss (1997), Francis and Schipper (1999), Brown, Lo, and Lys (1999).

References

Bernard, V. and K. Schipper, "Recognition and Disclosure in Financial Reporting," Unpublished paper, University of Michigan, November 1994.

Brown, S., K. Lo, and T. Lys. 1999. "Use of R^2 in Accounting Research: Measuring Changes in Value Relevance Over the Last Four Decades." *Journal of Accounting and Economics* 28, 2 (December): 83-115.

Collins, D. W., E. L. Maydew, and I. S. Weiss. 1999. "Changes in the Value-Relevance of Earnings and Book Values Over the Past Forty Years." *Journal of Accounting and Economics* 24: 39-67.

Francis, J., and K. Schipper. 1999. "Have Financial Statements Lost Their Relevance?" *Journal of Accounting Research* 37, 2 (Autumn): 319-352.

Holthausen, R. W., and R. L. Watts. 2001. "The Relevance of the Value-Relevance Literature for Financial Accounting Standard Setting." Draft dated March 29, 2001. Forthcoming in the *Journal of Accounting and Economics*. University of Pennsylvania and University of Rochester.

Leftwich, R. W. 1980. Market Failure Fallacies and Accounting Information. *Journal of Accounting and Economics* 2, 3 (December): 193-211.

Lev, B. 2001. *Intangibles: Management, Measurement, and Reporting*. Washington, D.C.: Brookings Institution Press.

Defined Terms

Business Combination Accounting   A set of formal guidelines describing how assets, liabilities, non-controlling interest, and goodwill must be reported by a purchasing company on its Consolidated Statement of Financial Position.[1]

Contingent Talent   Non-employees contracted directly or through an agency to perform work for a temporary period of time. Distinct from outsourced services, individuals are supervised by a company manager as if they were permanent employees, although being employees of the agent or self-employed.

Free Agent   Any worker who is not subject to full employment by a company; may be an individual practitioner who is working full-time or a temporary resource. All contingent talent is counted within the Free Agent description.

Human Capital   The present discounted value of the additional productivity over and above the product of skilled labor, of people with skills and qualifications.[2] Human capital is owned by those people.

Human Capital Formation   The process of adding to the supply of an enterprise's human capital, either by developing or by acquiring it from outside sources.

Intellectual Capital   Means of productivity derived from certain intangible assets; a subset of intangible assets.

Intellectual Property   Private property rights in ideas (for example, copyright and patents).[3]

Intangible Assets   Assets of an enterprise that cannot be seen or touched. These assets include goodwill, patents, trademarks, and copyright.[4]

Knowledge Worker   Executives, professionals and employees who know how to put knowledge to productive use; owns both the "means of production" and the "tools of production."[5]

Service Worker   Between knowledge worker and laborer (support, maintenance, clerical, and so on) is service worker; different from labor; machine serves worker.

Talent   People having the skills and abilities to fill specific professional roles.

Note

Terms are defined as used in the context of this book.

Endnotes

1. Investopedia.com, dictionary.
2. Oxford Dictionary of Economics, John Black, Oxford University Press, 1997.
3. Oxford Dictionary of Economics, John Black, Oxford University Press, 1997.
4. Oxford Dictionary of Economics, John Black, Oxford University Press, 1997.
5. Post-Capitalist Society, Peter Drucker, HarperBusiness 1993.

Index

Numbers

3M, 184
  talent supply
    director of international
      taxation, 87-88
    in-house search experts, 90-91
    marketing development
      manager, 89
    senior product support
      engineer, 88-89
    senior systems support
      managers, 86-87
  value-driven talent strategies, 69-70
10-K form, 41

A

advertising, 135
  Coca-Cola, 49-50
AFL-CIO, 151
algorithms
  IC (intellectual capital), 23
  ICI algorithm, 41
    company valuations, 29-30
  intellectual capital algorithm,
    Merck & Co., 55
Amgen, 148
analyzing
  companies within industries using
    IC%, 38-39
  individual companies over time, 40
Apple, iPods, 157-158
Archer-Daniels-Midland Company,
  37-38
areas of opportunity, 186
assessments, human capitalists,
  125-126

assets, 17-18
  intangible assets, 18-20, 56-57
    financial statements, 20-21
  potential impact of long-lived assets
    on IC calculation, 43-44
attributes that are important to
  investors, 136
awards, 133

B

bad hires, 164
banks, navigating oddities, 44
Beatles, equality of roles, 9-10
best practices, 160
biotech firms, 148
book value, 18, 22
borrow option, 79, 82, 94
  critical roles, 79
brand building, 185
brand equities, identifying, 136
  equivalent equities, 138
  key brand equities, 138
  potential strengths, 137-136
  potential vulnerabilities, 137
brand messages
  communicating, 138-139
  creating, 134-135
  gathering data from those you want
    to hire, 135
brand positioning, 133-136
brands
  building, 52-54
  employment brands, 128-130
  human capital, 52-54
Brands & Trademark Recognition,
  3M, 70

203

D

data
    collecting, for talent quality, 120-122
    sourcing for use in ICI calculations, 40-43
data elements, 41
debt, 93-94
debt-free market value, 22
decision trees, build, buy, or borrow, 79
Deep Segment Expertise, UPS, 73
designing, contingent talent, 98
developing, strategies, 170-172
director of international taxation, 87-88
disclosing, intellectual capital, 153-154
Disclosure of Information About Intangible Assets Not Recognized in Financial Statements, 149-152
disclosures, 68
discounted present value, 188
dividend payout, human capitalists, 124-125
Dow Jones Industrial Average, 142
Drucker, Peter, 53-54, 143

E

Elance-oDesk, 82
Element 1, David Ulrich model, 159
Element 2, David Ulrich model, 159
Element 3, David Ulrich model, 160
Element 4, David Ulrich model, 160
employment brand, 130
    taglines, 134
employment brand message, 128
employment engagement surveys, 177
employment life cycles, 130-132
    communicating throughout, 131
employment stints, human capitalists, 125-126
Enron, 152
enterprise value, 22
    versus intellectual capital, 29-30
equality of roles, 11-13
    Beatles, 9-10
    Coca-Cola, 7-11
equity, 93-94
equivalent equities, 138-139

external forces, 149
external hires, measuring quality, 118
Exxon Mobil, 45

F

Facebook, 164
FASB (Financial Accounting Standards Board), 19, 149-150
Fast Company magazine, 163
Finance, 169
    HR and, 169-170
finance, 6
Financial Accounting Standards Board (FASB), 19
financial capital, 93-94
    borrow option, 94
    versus human capital, 94
financial services firms, navigating oddities, 44
financial statements, intangible assets, 20-21
Form 10-K, 41
free agents, 82
Freedman, Milton, 5, 190
FTE (full-time equivalent employee), 92
full-time equivalent employee (FTE), 92
future of HR (human resources), 168-169

G

Gillette Business, 22, 34
Glassdoor, 124
Global Reporting Initiative (GRI), 152
goodwill, Gillette Business, 36
Google, 66, 164
GRI (Global Reporting Initiative), 152
growth of intellectual capital, 47-48
Groysberg, Boris, 107

H

halo effect, employment brand, 128-129
hiring mission critical roles, 50
Hoffman, Reid, 124
The Home Depot, Merchants, 81